# FASCISM

## Martin Kitchen

*Associate Professor of History,*
*Simon Fraser University*

palgrave

Reprinted 1985, 1990, 1994

Published by
PALGRAVE
Houndmills, Basingstoke, Hampshire RG21 6XS and
175 Fifth Avenue, New York, N.Y. 10010
Companies and representatives throughout the world

PALGRAVE is the new global academic imprint of
St. Martin's Press LLC Scholarly and Reference Division and
Palgrave Publishers Ltd (formerly Macmillan Press Ltd).

ISBN 0–333–18591–9 hardcover
ISBN 0–333–18592–7 paperback

This book is printed on paper suitable for recycling and
made from fully managed and sustained forest sources.

A catalogue record for this book is available
from the British Library.

10   9   8   7   6   5   4   3
08   07   06   05   04   03   02   01

Printed and bound in Great Britain by
Antony Rowe Ltd, Eastbourne

Transferred to digital printing 2001

In memoriam Wilhelm Meyer

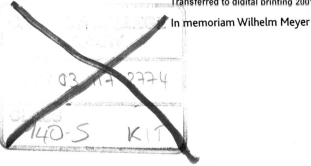

# Contents

# Acknowledgements

I am greatly indebted to the Canada Council for their generous support, without which this book could not have been written. I should also like to record my thanks to the Istituto Italiano di Cultura in London both for the excellence of their language instruction and for bibliographical assistance. To Signora Maria Rosa Maranzano I owe a special debt of gratitude. Tim Mason and Ralph Miliband made many valuable criticisms of the manuscript, and their efforts have resulted in many improvements. The shortcomings that remain are entirely my own. I am also very grateful for the friendly encouragement of Shaie Selzer. Lastly my thanks are due to my wife for her incisive criticisms and unfailing assistance.

# Introduction

The word 'fascism' has always been subject to many different definitions, and recently it has degenerated into a simple term of abuse. To denounce as 'fascist' military dictatorships in Latin America, regimes in the under-developed countries, the practices of the Metropolitan Police Force, or restrictions on the rights and freedoms of homosexuals, may well provide a strong rallying cry and excite a powerful response, but it does nothing to uncover the true nature of the problems under attack.

Some, particularly on the left, would argue that this does not matter. Using as a sacred text Marx's well-known eighth thesis on Feuerbach, they quote: 'All social life is essentially *practical*. All mysteries that induce theory to mysticism find their rational solution in human practice and in the conception of this practice.'* By an undialectical and narrow reading of the Marxist concept of practice such people would argue that any attempt to formulate a general theory of fascism would be essentially reactionary, fatalistic and idealistic. Refusing to accept that consciousness can direct and inform the objective reality of practice, it is felt that practice alone can provide an absolute criterion of truth. The proof of the pudding is in the eating. Such a view has a certain common-sense appeal. It calls for action rather than introspection, it appeals to the heart rather than the mind. How much better to concentrate on attacking some vicious and cruel regime of the extreme right than worry all the time whether or not it is fascist. Such an argument, however, is the result of a misunderstanding of the role of theory in politics. There is no simple alternative of theory or practice, the two must be intertwined. Theory should illuminate and guide practice, which in turn must correct and test theory. The history of the theories of fascism provides sorry instances of what happens when this dialectical relationship is not established. There

* *Marx Engels Werke*, vol. 3 (Berlin, 1969) p. 7.

were times when experience provided the correct answer, but fatally late – the insight was thus of limited practical value. Conversely the etiquette 'fascist' was awarded to movements that were not fascist at all, so that no adequate defence against the real fascists was possible. Theory must therefore attempt to discover the ingredients of a social movement before it becomes lethal, and it must distinguish between various different sorts of dangerous political movement so that adequate antidotes may be found. Above all, theory must take cognisance of the immense complexity of social movements, and must therefore be flexible and many-sided so as not to reduce the complex to an over-simplified formula. When all these considerations are taken into account theory becomes a powerful political weapon, a guide to action, and a means to critical insight into social forces which may not be immediately apparent. Correct typology of social movements, far from limiting and inhibiting political action, should extend its scope and its effectiveness. A thing does not have to be fascist to be bad, but if fascism is made synonymous with badness it must be by very definition. Such confusion as this seriously weakened the anti-fascist struggle in the inter-war years, and without a clear understanding of the nature of fascism the fight against fascistoid tendencies in the present day will be beset with similar problems.

The attempt to provide an operational definition of fascism can thus be justified as a way of giving back to the term 'fascism' some clear meaning which it has lost, and as an aid to the combating of fascist tendencies in the present day. But it is also important from a more purely scientific point of view. The vast number of individual studies on fascism and the compilation of empirical data need now to be informed and integrated by theoretical discussion. The weaknesses and shortcomings of existing theories of fascism need to be pointed out so that advances can be made in the understanding of the phenomenon. Theory can also help to bring together the different disciplines which have addressed themselves to the problem of fascism. Sociology, psychology, political science and history need to be confronted with the detailed researches of other disciplines, and theory can thus integrate individual efforts so that real progress can be made in the analysis and the debate on the origins, function and *telos* of fascism.

If it is agreed that a discussion of theories of fascism is necessary for all these reasons, the vexed question remains as to how narrow or how wide the definition is to be. This is a very real problem in the social sciences, and one to which insufficient attention has been paid. If a theory is too narrow it becomes almost tautological, but if it is too wide it has little heuristic value. It is still a commonly held view that the term 'fascism' can only be applied to Mussolini's regime in Italy, and that it is inadmissible to use it to describe Hitler's Germany. Other writers go even further and claim that fascism never existed at all, it was simply part of a wider movement called 'totalitarianism'; or they try to discount fascism altogether by writing it off as 'Hitlerism' – hence the spate of biographies of Hitler which all too often serve to disguise and conceal the true nature of fascism. The term 'fascism' must be wide enough to apply to a number of similar movements without becoming so broad that it loses all meaning. In the same way 'theory' must also be seen in an undogmatic and comprehensive sense of that which goes beyond the mere compilation of facts and the reconstruction of the past or the present to make certain generalisations, axioms and statements on the nature of fascism without having to pretend to be comprehensive or final.

After the First World War there were movements in almost all European states which showed distinct fascist tendencies. They rejected the idea of parliamentary democracy. They opposed the organised working class and the philosophy of socialism. They were violently nationalistic. They subscribed to a vague anti-capitalism. They preached submission to authority, discipline and an irrational sense of community. At first they were small and cranky sects, and some of them fortunately remained so. In 1922 the fascists seized power in Italy, and after 1929 and the Great Depression an enormous impetus was given to fascist movements, and in 1933 Hitler was able to establish the most radical and brutal of fascist regimes.

When fascism ceased to be an eccentric movement of the extreme right and became a force that could no longer be ignored, an increasing number of attempts were made to provide a theoretical explanation of the phenomenon. A bewildering number of theories were produced which examined fascism from many different political standpoints and which emphasised particular characteristics of fascism.

Ernst Nolte has attempted to order the numerous theories of fascism under six different headings. Christian theorists see fascism as the result of the secularisation of a society which turns away from God; but this theory implies that the antidote to fascism is some form of theocracy. Conservatives see fascism as a revolt by the masses against traditional values which are beginning to totter under the strain of social and economic change; they therefore yearn for a return to the 'good old days' with a certain pessimistic nostalgia. Liberals see fascism as a form of totalitarianism, and as a result they are unable to make a proper distinction between fascism and Stalinism. Nationalists look upon fascism as either the high or the low point in national history, and thus either support fascism, or share the conservatives' nostalgia for earlier times. Marxists see fascism resulting from the contradictions within advanced capitalism, and thus argue that the abolition of capitalist society is, in the last resort, the only effective antidote to fascism. Lastly, Nolte trundles out his own 'nonpartisan' theory, for which he makes the extravagant claim that by seeing fascism as a specific and supra-national phenomenon of a particular epoch a way can be found to discard the burden of the past and a path opened to a solution of the problems of the moment.

Nolte's classification of theories of fascism is helpful, but this book is mainly concerned with those theories of fascism which stress the social basis and the social function of fascism, although the two most influential approaches of the post-war era – the theory of totalitarianism and Ernst Nolte's own work – are also discussed. In place of Nolte's six-fold classification, theories of fascism are placed under two general headings. Theories which assert that fascism is determined and produced by capitalism (or, to use the somewhat euphemistic terms, 'industrial society', 'modern society', 'the age of the masses' or 'modernisation') are contrasted with theories which hold that fascism was an independent force which was able to determine the course of capitalist development. The first group of theories are labelled 'heteronomic' and the second 'autonomic' theories of fascism. The extreme form of the heteronomic theory is that evolved by the Third International, which saw the fascists as the agents of monopoly capitalism. The autonomic theory finds its most popular expression in the theory that fascism was an independent movement of the uprooted and alienated middle classes. At the end of the book it is argued that an adequate theory of fascism must combine elements of both the heteronomic and the autonomic theories. This approach is described as a 'syncretic' theory of fascism.

Examples of fascist practice are taken from Italy and Germany, particularly the latter, for these are cases of the fascist maximum. By discussing Italy and Germany the danger of being side-tracked into discussing whether or not the particular regime under discussion was or was not fascist, whether it was fascistoid or merely ultra-conservative, is avoided. Both regimes provide the best material for discussing the structure, function, causes and dynamics of fascism. By approaching the problem in this way it is hoped that a distinction will become apparent between fascism and other forms of exceptional state power, such as military dictatorship, Bonapartism, or oligarchy.

The theme of this book is the relationship between social structure and fascism. It is argued that fascism, as a social movement, must be socially determined and is not produced by the peculiarities of 'national character', by the quirks of history, by accident, by the manipulations of Pied Pipers or cliques of sinister plotters, by the fantasies of the mind, or even worse, the genitals. Fascism is the product of a society which blocks the further development of the genuine freedom of mankind and which is determined to maintain outmoded and irrational modes of production. The problem of fascism is thus not of mere historical interest. The study of fascism and the theories which have been developed to explain it should direct our attention to fascist tendencies in contemporary society, and should strengthen the determination to work for the emancipation of society from the burdens of the past and direct and indirect repression in the present. Inasmuch as this is possible the scientific examination of the social can free man from the shackles of the past and guide his action in the present, thus establishing the true relationship between theory and practice. That this remains an ideal which, with our shortcomings and weakness, we are unable to achieve, should not discourage the attempt. There is more at stake than a mere problem of semantics.

# Chapter 1

# The Third International and Fascism

At the last world congress of the Communist International which was attended by Lenin, the Fourth Congress held in 1922, the first comments on fascism were made. A few days after Mussolini's 'March on Rome' the International issued a manifesto to the Italian workers. The Italian party was blamed in part for the rise of fascism by its failure to pursue a revolutionary policy, and it was argued that revolutionary action was still possible. The fascist movement was seen as 'primarily a weapon in the hands of the big landowners', supported by some workers as well as peasants and *déclassé* elements. The industrial and commercial bourgeoisie were said to be disturbed by the actions of this 'black bolshevism'.

The extraordinary theoretical confusion of this first statement, due in part to a refusal to accept Mussolini's break with the 'rural fascism' of Grandi and the 'left' fascism of Farinacci in 1921 as sincere, and the inability to analyse the tremendous support given to the fascists by big capital, was partly corrected in the course of the conference. In the theses on tactics, published four weeks later, it was stated that fascism was an offensive by the bourgeoisie against the working class, made possible by the collaborationist policies of the social democrats and the failure of the communists to exploit the weakness of post-war capitalism. The crisis was seen as 'objectively revolutionary' and therefore greater militancy was demanded. There was no mention of the role of the landowners. The main danger was felt to be the ability of the fascists to gain a footing among the masses. This fact, combined with its counter-revolutionary fighting organisations, was deemed to be the characteristic feature of 'classic' fascism. For their alleged complicity with fascism the social democrats were dubbed 'social traitors'.

The attitude of the Fourth Congress was due in large part to the arguments of the left-wing Italian communist leader, Bordiga. In the following year Gramsci visited Moscow and gave a more subtle and profound account of the nature of Italian fascism, although he, like his comrade Angelo Tasca, tended to exaggerate the rural nature of fascism. The German communist Clara Zetkin insisted that the key to fascism was its ability to attract a mass following of hungry, suffering, disappropriated and disappointed men who, if fascism was to be halted, would have to be won over to the communist camp, or at least politically neutralised. Clara Zetkin was sharply critical of those communists who saw fascism simply as a terrorist movement, and insisted that before fascism resorted to terror it had already won a political and ideological victory over the labour movement. Karl Radek, whose brilliance as a debater enlivened many of the early discussions on fascism within the International, argued that communists should be prepared to use nationalism to win the masses away from the right. For Radek the nationalism of a large section of the petit bourgeoisie and the intelligentsia was due to a desire to escape from the depressing realities of the present. Big capitalists and landowners, who were largely responsible for the plight of the masses, were able to organise and manipulate them for their own ends. Seen in these terms fascism, to Radek, was the 'socialism of the petit bourgeois masses'.

Some of these criticisms of the Fourth Congress were incorporated into the resolution of the Third Executive Committee of the Communist International (E.C.C.I.) Plenum on fascism in 1923. Greater emphasis was placed on the mass following of the fascist movements, but this was blamed in large part on the perfidy of the 'social traitors' who had robbed the radicalised petit bourgeoisie of the belief that the working class was the 'mighty agent of radical social transformation'. Whereas at the Fourth Congress fascism was seen as the 'weakest counter-revolutionary organisation in existence', this new emphasis on its mass base was a step away from such left-wing confidence, but the belief was still widespread that fascism was a temporary form of domination at a time of imminent capitalist collapse.

At the Fifth Congress in 1924 Bordiga was again the main speaker and the resolution on fascism adopted by the Congress marks a step back. Fascism was seen as 'one of the classic forms of counter-revolution in the epoch when capitalist society is decaying, the epoch of proletarian revolution'. The resolution noted that the social origin of the fascist mass movement was in the middle classes, who were doomed to decay as a result of the economic and social crisis, and those whose revolutionary hopes had been dashed. With the remorseless decline of bourgeois society more and more bourgeois parties take on a fascist character. This is particularly true of social democracy. Thus: 'Fascism and social democracy are the two sides of the same instrument of capitalist dictatorship. In the fight against fascism, therefore, social democracy can never be a reliable ally of the fighting proletariat.' The introduction to the resolution ends with another pious incantation of the Comintern's belief that because of its internal contradictions fascism immediately becomes politically bankrupt and disintegrates. In his speech Bordiga specifically rejected Clara Zetkin's emphasis on the strength of the fascist mass movement, and insisted that it was largely a paid mercenary force in the service of the bourgeoisie, with little autonomous power or ambition.

Although the debate on the nature of fascism continued within the international, and some contributions of real merit were made, it was not until the Sixth Congress in 1928 that a new set of theses was published. The Congress marks the highest point of the Comintern's analysis of fascism as directly caused by capitalism and the capitalist elite, and thus as a heteronomous force. This view was almost taken to the extreme of actually identifying capitalism with fascism. Fascism was seen as a means of bourgeois domination that was not marked by a new or even drastically modified form of state organisation. The main characteristic of fascism is that the bourgeoisie exercises direct power independent from the 'relations and combinations between the parties', and disguises this direct rule with the ideology of class collaboration, 'which is the official social-democratic ideology of fascism'. A fascist is one who attempts in any way to suppress or control the class struggle of the militant communist proletariat. Seen in these terms there was little objective difference between the social democrats and the fascists. As early as 1924 Stalin had written that: 'Social democracy is objectively the moderate wing of fascism. . . . These two organisations are not contradictory, they complement one another. They are not antipodes, but twin brothers.' At the Sixth Congress Stalin demanded an all-out attack on social democracy,

which had ceased to be a shamefaced defender and apologist for capitalism and had become its active supporter, and he silenced those on the
right of the International, like Bucharin and Togliatti, who felt that in
the face of a mounting fascist menace the communists should collaborate
with the social democrats and at the same time strive for a scientific
understanding of fascism rather than be content with mere agitation.

Along with this clear articulation of the theory of 'social fascism',
which had been implicit in Comintern thinking since 1922, the Sixth
Congress also reaffirmed the idea that fascism was a defensive measure by
the bourgeoisie, an expression of its frustration and weakness and a direct
result of the economic crisis. Fascism was seen as the counterpart to
revolutionary proletarian activity and the maturing revolutionary situation. Fascism was also chronologically the final phase of capitalism, not
the 'qualitatively highest form' as Clara Zetkin had insisted, and as
Dimitroff was later to argue. Thus fascism was seen as a necessary final
stage in the transition from capitalism to socialism.

The resolutions of the Sixth Congress mark the beginning of the 'third
period' of the Communist International, which was to last until 1935 and
which provides a depressing example of the effects of faulty theoretical
understanding on political practice. The theory of 'social fascism' made
it impossible for there to be any united working-class effort against fascism. The Tenth Plenum of the E.C.C.I. announced that 'in countries
where there are strong social democratic parties, fascism assumes the particular form of social fascism, which is ever-increasing in the extent to
which it serves the bourgeoisie as an instrument for the paralysing of the
activity of the masses in the struggle against the regime of fascist dictatorship'. In its worst form this could lead to the belief that the struggle
against social democracy was even more important than the struggle
against fascism. The resolutions also came perilously close to asserting
that fascism was inevitable, just as Bordiga had asserted on behalf of his
party in 1922 that fascism was the inescapable consequence of the development of capitalism. Indeed it could almost be argued that fascism was
desirable in that it was an unpleasant but unavoidable step on the road to
socialism. Lastly, the confusing of bourgeois presidential regimes, like
that of Brüning in Germany (1930–2), with fascism had a disastrous
effect on the struggle against National Socialism, for according to the
Sixth Congress there could be no essential difference between a regime
headed by Brüning or by Hitler.

During the 'third period' Manuilsky continued to hammer home the thesis that social fascism was the key to the nature of fascism. At the Eleventh E.C.C.I. Plenum in 1931 he said:

> The fascist regime is not a new type of state; it is a form of the bourgeois dictatorship in the epoch of imperialism. It grows organically out of bourgeois democracy. . . . Only a bourgeois liberal can accept that there is a contradiction between bourgeois democracy and a fascist regime, that these two political forms are different in principle; by constructing such a contradiction, social democracy is deliberately deceiving the masses.

Fascist ideas about industrial peace and democracy were taken directly from social democracy. 'This common ideology is the best proof of the kinship of fascism and social fascism.' In his conclusion Manuilsky said:

> Our definition does not place fascism in the position of a deciding factor of the revolutionary crisis, but allocates it the modest role of one of the symptoms of the disorientation of the ruling classes and of their endeavour to find a way out of the position by the suppression of the working class. . . . Fascism is not a new method of rule distinct from the whole system of bourgeois dictatorship. Whoever thinks that is a liberal.

The effect of such a theory on political practice can be clearly demonstrated by Thaelmann's report on the situation in Germany. The German communist party (K.P.D.) had succeeded 'in bringing the advance of fascism to a halt, and in bringing about a certain stagnation, indeed the first beginnings of a decline in the national socialist movement'. Thaelmann insisted that the para-military organisation of the social democrats (S.P.D.) was not designed to fight fascism, but rather to crush the revolutionary proletariat in the interests of the capitalists. At a meeting of the central committee of the German party in February 1932 Thaelmann warned against an 'opportunist over-estimation of Hitler-fascism', and insisted that the struggle against fascism should be combined with a strategy, the main aim of which was the struggle against social democracy.

In the course of 1932 the ever-growing menace of German fascism forced the International to modify its position. At the twelfth plenary session of the E.C.C.I. Manuilsky denounced those fatalists in the communist movement who felt that: 'The historic task of preparing the proletarian revolution will be carried out for us by war and fascism, that

war and fascism will undermine and destroy the influence of social
democracy which is the main obstacle in the path of proletarian revolution.' At a meeting of the central committee of the K.P.D. in May
Thaelmann argued that the Stalinist theory of the 'twin brothers' was
false (he had made a very tentative step in this direction at the Eleventh
E.C.C.I. Plenum) and stressed the different social composition of the
S.P.D. and the N.S.D.A.P. (Nationalsozialistische Deutsche Arbeiter-
partei – Nazis). But the K.P.D. still refused any bloc politics with the
leadership of the 'social fascists'. As it was still believed that the social
democrats provided the mass base for fascism, the main effort of the
K.P.D. was still directed at destroying the social fascist leadership and
winning over the rank and file to the struggle against fascism. At the
same time Thaelmann warned that the struggle against social democracy
should not be used as an excuse to ignore the struggle against fascism, a
point which was taken up by Kuusinen at the Twelfth E.C.C.I. Plenum.
The International still seemed to be blind to the true dangers of German
fascism. Togliatti was almost alone in warning that the situation was so
critical that something more than the old social fascist clichés was needed
to deal with the danger.

   The appointment of Hitler as chancellor was taken as triumphant
proof of the theory of social fascism. For all its talk about the struggle
against fascism the K.P.D. regarded the S.P.D. as the 'main social support for the dictatorship of capital', and the destruction of social fascism
remained the main task, so that the decline and collapse of fascism could
be followed by the dictatorship of the proletariat. Not even the massive
persecution of the 'twin brother of Nazi-fascism' made the K.P.D.
change its line. The argument that the revolutionary forces in Germany had suffered a set-back was denounced as opportunist and capitu-
latory.

   At the thirteenth plenary session of the E.C.C.I. the dissident German
communists Remmele and Neumann were denounced for claiming that
fascism stood in contradiction to bourgeois democracy and meant a
change in the organisation of the capitalist state. Wilhelm Pieck's criticism of Remmele and Neumann was a little more subtle. He argued that
their mistake had been to imagine that fascism was a dictatorship of the
lumpenproletariat, a variation of a view he ascribed to Trotsky and
Bauer that it was the dictatorship of the petit bourgeoisie. He also
pointed out that the only force that could stop fascism was the united
working class, but the S.P.D. had such a fatal effect on the masses that

this was not possible. Although Pieck still supported the Stalinist theory of the twins, there is clear indication that the International was beginning to take a closer look at the class basis of fascism and was looking at it in a less schematic manner. Nevertheless the debates were marked by familiar polemics against the social fascists and by a tragically ludicrous revolutionary optimism. Kuusinen called Trotsky's remark that it was not the proletarian revolution that was maturing in Germany, but rather the fascist counter-revolution which was deepening, 'Trotsky's Horst Wessel Song'.

As far as the theory of fascism is concerned the most important step taken at the Thirteenth Plenum was the publication of the thesis which still remains the basis of Marxist-Leninist definitions of fascism. 'Fascism is the open, terrorist dictatorship of the most reactionary, most chauvinist and most imperialist elements of finance capital.' Although this definition was clearly in need of refinement, it did mark a step forward in that it made a clear distinction between fascism and bourgeois liberalism, even if the distinction was still largely one of degree, and it also opened the way towards the formation of a broad anti-fascist alliance. But before this could be achieved the social fascist polemics would have to be dropped.

It was Georgi Dimitroff who, at the Seventh Congress of the Comintern in 1935, delivered the death-blow to the theory of fascism of the 'third period', and in his lengthy report provided the basis for all further discussions of fascism in the communist parties and the scientific investigations of fascism by scholars in the socialist countries. As early as 1934, when Dimitroff began his work on the report, he realised that the theory of fascism was a 'barricade on our way towards the social democratic workers'. He was sharply critical of the belief that the social democrats were the main support of the bourgeoisie, and that their left wing was a particular danger. He realised that the 'united front from below' was little more than a tactic to expose the social democratic leadership, and that what was wanted was a genuine anti-fascist united front which implied a real co-operation with the social democratic leadership and a reform of the 'heavy-handed bureaucratic apparatus of the E.C.C.I.'.

Dimitroff's report to the Congress was a startling repudiation of the Comintern's theory of fascism. His starting point was the definition provided by the Thirteenth Plenum, which led him to assert that 'fascism is the power of finance capital itself', and thus to reject all theories of fascism as standing above the classes or being a dictatorship of the petit bourgeoisie or the lumpenproletariat. At the same time he repudiated the theory of the Sixth Congress, saying: 'The accession to power of fascism is not an ordinary succession of one bourgeois government by another, but a substitution of one state form of class domination of the bourgeoisie – bourgeois democracy – by another form – open terrorist dictatorship.' Thus the struggle for the preservation of liberties within the bourgeois state must form an important part of the struggle against fascism. The widespread belief in the International that capitalism and fascism were identical was also criticised by Dimitroff, in that such a belief was both absurd in itself and made a coalition with other anti-fascist forces impossible. By defining fascism as the dictatorship of the most reactionary elements of finance capital it was seen as qualitatively the 'last' stage of capitalism, but not necessarily a stage through which all capitalist states would have to go before becoming socialist. On the other hand, fascism is unable to halt the disintegration of capitalism, for it helps to form an alliance of those revolutionary elements who reject the policy of class collaboration and who are bound to serve as the grave-diggers of capitalism.

The fatal error of the Comintern during the 'Third Period' was its failure to articulate a mass line. The theory of social fascism served to cut the communist parties off from the masses and to leave them ineffective against the fascist menace. This was partly corrected at the Seventh Congress and the new popular front policy was to have several successes, even though it was often almost impossible to heal old and deep wounds caused by years of denouncing many anti-fascists as twin brothers of fascism. The admission that fascism was a different form of the bourgeois capitalist state was both scientifically correct and politically wise, for whereas fascist states destroyed the labour movement, in the 'normal' capitalist state the labour movement could organise and prepare for the defence of those bourgeois liberties which had previously been denounced as fraudulent, but which were now seen to be ideas for which a broad anti-fascist front would be prepared to fight. The Comintern was also slowly beginning to realise that social democratic parties, with their large working-class base, could not simply be used and manipulated by fiendishly cunning monopoly capitalists. For all their class-collaborationist policies they could never become fully independent of their class base.

Certain other misconceptions were also clarified. Until the rise of

Hitler the fact that fascism was the outcome of the imperialist stage of capitalism, according to Lenin's familiar definition of imperialism, had not been adequately analysed, and for all the talk of fascism as a phenomenon created by the final stages of capitalism there was a tendency to think of fascism as a political movement in relatively backward countries. Dimitroff correctly stressed the chauvinist and predatory nature of fascism and argued that it was likely to mount a crusade against the Soviet Union. Yet a number of serious misconceptions still remained. The International still thought that fascism was the result of a general economic crisis which was all too easily equated with a revolutionary situation and a proletarian offensive. Seen in these terms fascism was a defensive action by monopoly capitalism in response to growing proletarian militancy or, in Dimitroff's terms, a counter-offensive. In fact fascism was an offensive by capitalist forces which followed significant working-class defeats. For all the problems facing capitalist society and the perceptions of danger to the established system from the militant working class, the political crisis within the ranks of the bourgeoisie was combined with an offensive strategy which demonstrated the relative strength of the bourgeoisie against the proletariat. At the Seventh Congress Dimitroff only hinted that the rise of fascism occurred at a time when the working class was forced on the defensive, but it needs considerable textual exegesis to extract this point.

The consequence of the failure to understand the extent to which the working class had suffered defeats and had been forced on the defensive was an excessive optimism that fascism would soon collapse as a result of its internal contradictions. Here the Comintern's analysis was once again marred by an undialectical economism. Just as economic crisis was equated with a developing revolutionary situation, so fascism was doomed because of the contradictions within the system. Clara Zetkin had been almost alone in stressing the way in which fascism had enabled the creation of an alliance between the big bourgeoisie and the petit bourgeoisie which, with all its internal contradictions, was extraordinarily powerful. The Comintern failed to see the importance of the mass base of fascism and thus underestimated both its offensive strength and its staying power. Greater emphasis on the mass base of fascism would also have prevented the Comintern from thinking of fascist movements as being little more than the paid agents of monopoly capitalism with virtually no autonomy. Regardless of the fact that this view was difficult to reconcile with the insistence on the 'internal contradictions' within fascism, it was a strikingly crude example of vulgar-Marxist determinist economism, which denied Marx's insistence on the dialectical relationship between basis and superstructure and which reduced dialectical materialism to a mono-causal determinism.

Dimitroff's speech to the Seventh Congress remains the basis of the present-day Marxist-Leninist heteronomic theory of fascism. Fascism is seen as an essentially dependent movement, for fascists are the agents of monopoly capitalism with little autonomous will. The problem with this theory is to provide adequate empirical data on the ways in which big capital dominated the fascist movement. In the course of searching for such data much valuable historical material has been uncovered, particularly by historians in East Germany, which establishes beyond any reasonable doubt the close connections between big industry and fascism. Although the agent theory imposes a severe restriction on the development of a scientific examination of fascism, many Marxist-Leninist authors have produced works of considerable value which employ a more subtle operationalisation of the relationships between capital and fascism, and which also examine the differing interests and political stances within monopoly capitalism itself. However, this heteronomic theory makes it exceptionally hard to uncover the dynamics behind fascist policy, particularly in foreign affairs. Imperialism, aggressive war, the attack on the Soviet Union, and even the military strategy employed, can all be seen in terms of the problems of monopoly capitalism and capitalist reproduction, but the precise relationship between fascist decision-making in these areas and the overall political conception of fascism with that of the representatives of monopoly capitalism remains obscure. The 'agent theory' is unable to expose the transmission belts between the monopoly capitalists and their agents.

Yet for all its shortcomings as a theory of fascism, and in spite of the unfortunate political consequences, the Third International's discussion of fascism was not without its strong points. Compared to discussions of fascism among bourgeois intellectuals it was a considerable achievement, and the weaknesses of the theory are due in large part to the exceptionally difficult political circumstances in which it was developed. By stressing the relationship between capitalism and fascism, however dogmatically and schematically, the communists were very much on the right lines, and their work could be more fruitfully developed than the notions of fascism as the dictatorship of the middle classes, or vague and unsystematic discussions of fascist ideology. Stripped of their dogmatism and enriched with a truly dialectical understanding of the social process, the theses of the Seventh Congress provide a worthwhile starting point for an examination of the nature of fascism.

# Chapter 2

# Psychological Theories of Fascism

The sadistic behaviour of fascist gangs, the extraordinary mass hysteria generated by fascist rallies, and the apparently pathological conduct of many fascist leaders seemed to be such striking characteristics of fascist regimes that it was widely assumed that psychology was the only discipline capable of providing an adequate explanation of fascism. Social psychologists saw fascism and anti-semitism as a fruitful area for fresh research and speculation, or as confirmation of their fondly held theories. The gloomy prophets of 'mass society' saw in fascism the realisation of their worst fears that bourgeois culture, which in their view was synonymous with civilisation itself, would be drowned in the irrational, brutal, instinctual and easily manipulated behaviour of the masses. From the other end of the political spectrum neo-Marxists were anxious to discover the mechanisms whereby the economic infrastructure was reflected in the ideological superstructure, so that the relationship between social being and consciousness could be established and the origins of 'false consciousness' illuminated.

As early as 1933 Harold Lasswell realised that the psychological aspects of fascism were firmly rooted within a complex of economic, historical and social forces. In a preliminary essay on the 'Psychology of Hitlerism' he stressed that the mass appeal of fascism was part of a desperate reaction by the lower middle class in which anti-semitism played a critical functional role in uniting the petit bourgeoisie and the aristocracy against 'Jewish capitalism'. The upper bourgeoisie had thus been able to manipulate these feelings to destroy collective bargaining, and Lasswell admitted that 'the abandonment of so many of the forms of democratic government has corroborated the communist teaching that such trifles will be cast away whenever the class struggle seems to render it imperative for the protection of the profits principle'.

In the same year that Lasswell was attempting to uncover the social origins of fascist psychology, Wilhelm Reich published *The Mass Psychology of Fascism*, an extraordinary book which combines brilliant insights with passages of pure nonsense and which remains a work which still excites lively interest. Reich's main concern in this book was to discover why people were misled, why they suffered from false consciousness. He was thus attempting to add a psychological dimension to Marxist thought which would be capable of explaining the subjective factors in history. Needless to say the German communists were unimpressed by these attempts, and Reich was expelled from the party. Reich's answer was that false consciousness was directly caused by sexual inhibition, caused in turn by the repressive forces of the authoritarian family which was thus the factory of the authoritarian state's structure and ideology. Whereas Freud had argued that sexuality had to be repressed in the interests of civilisation and culture, Reich argued that infant masturbation and the sexual intercourse of adolescents did not interfere with the building of airplanes and gasolene stations. He argued that: 'Orgone biophysics has shown that the Freudian unconscious, the antisocial element in the human structure, is a secondary result of the repression of primary biological impulses' (p. vii).

The authority of the father requires strict sexual inhibition on the part of women and children, authoritarianism and nationalism were a continuation of these warped family ties, and imperialism was grounded in 'family imperialism' – the rivalry between different families. Basing his arguments on the works of Morgan and Engels he insisted that sexual repression had played an essential part in the formation of class society. Such repression blocked the way to rational thinking, formed the basis of religious beliefs, and culminated in the totalitarian regimes of the twentieth century. Thus 'Fascism is the result of thousands of years of warping of the human structure'. 'Humanity is biologically sick, politics the expression of this sickness' (p. 273). Man becomes a machine, moves away from animality and away from genitality, and this for Reich was a far more important cause of fascism than the economic motives on which the Marxists insisted. Fascism is the expression of the mechanistic–mystical character of man, a representation of the 'second character layer', and the result of 'biological rigidity'.

Since fascism was, in Reich's view, an authoritarian, one-party system, a totalitarian state based in large part on sexual repression, the Soviet Union was also fascistic in its Stalinist deformation. Reich was thus one of the earliest protagonists of the theory of totalitarianism, seeing in fascism one expression of the massive threat to democracy and freedom facing modern man. Reich was also one of the first to realise that there was a fundamental contradiction between the petit bourgeois anti-modern and anti-capitalist demands of the mass following of fascist regimes and the actual policies of the regimes which always favoured big capital. But he did not expect this to lead to the collapse of the regimes. He knew that the only effective challenge to fascism would have to come from the working class, but he feared that working class parties had been weakened by 'sex moralistic adaptation to the conservative middle class' (p. 62). His long-term aim was the abolition of the state and of politics and the realisation of 'work democracy' in which men could be free, responsible and fully human. The answer lay in 'sexual politics', which would liberate mankind and destroy the very foundations of fascism and totalitarianism. Yet this programme, which can be best summed up in the lapidary injunction of the 1960s, 'fuck for peace', although rightly stressing the importance of sexual inhibition as a factor in social control, was politically frivolous, and in his last years Reich warned against the 'pornographic, filthy, sick mind of man in sexual matters'.

The most important and rewarding book on the problem of fascism by a psychologist is undoubtedly Erich Fromm's *Escape from Freedom*, first published in 1941. His starting point is the early writings of Marx, in which Marx discusses the relationships between individual man and his environment, the problems of alienation, and where he lays the groundwork for a humanist sociology. Fromm concluded from his study of Marx that history was not the result of psychological forces, but at the same time the human factor could not simply be ignored, as it was by so many economistic vulgar-Marxists in the Third International. Thus he rejected Freud's belief in fixed instinctual drives which have the effect of making the relationship between man and society static, and argued with Marx that man's nature is a social product and that man's adaptation to culture is dynamic.

For Fromm fascism resulted from the alienation of man in the modern world, an expression of the fears and anxieties of those who had lost their way. In feudal society, to which Fromm attaches the label 'pre-individualistic society', the primary ties of clan, church, caste and family were particularly strong. From Marx he took the idea that feudal society combined vicious exploitation with a strong feeling of solidarity which saw existing society as a natural order, or in Fromm's parlance individual personality structures were attuned to the social order. With the growth of capitalism and the protestant Reformation this umbilical cord between the individual and society was cut, and man was given an enormous increase in freedom although the primary ties were broken. Man became the subject of economic life, but also the instrument of economic power, the prey to commodity fetishism and alienation. Man now became caught in the dialectical relationship between freedom and fear of that freedom. With the development of monopoly capitalist conditions this situation became further aggravated. The individual workers became anonymous cogs in vast corporate machines. The economic situation of the petit bourgeoisie was severely threatened. Society appeared to be so vast and impersonal that it could no longer be comprehended. The two popular figures of this new age were Nietzsche's superman who can soar above the daily world, and Mickey Mouse, the small and lovable creature who manages to escape some ghastly fate at the very last moment.

These widespread feelings of uncertainty and anxiety are not the result of society becoming neurotic, as some of the earlier psychologists had insisted, for only the individual can be neurotic, not society as a whole. Nor can Fromm accept the Freudian contention that capitalism is an expression of anal eroticism, for there is no adequate explanation for the specifically 'anal' characteristics of the European lower middle class. It is rather that society is organised in such a way that it is adverse to human happiness and self-realisation. Authoritarianism is part of the search for new secondary bonds to replace the primary bonds which have been lost. The fact that the human basis of fascism is found in the sado-masochistic authoritarian personality is due, according to Fromm, to the particular aggressiveness of a lower middle class which is isolated and threatened. Fascist ideology appeals to the extent to which it appears to offer answers to the human needs prominent in a given social character. Fascism is thus not something within the human soul as Mumford and others had argued,* nor is it the result of the sinister trickery of a fiendish group of monopoly capitalists; it is an attempt to rediscover the primary bonds which linked the individual to his world, but it is also an attempt which is bound to fail because in its profound anti-humanism it cannot lead to a union with the world. Hitler understood this aspect of fascism very well when he wrote: 'Idealism alone leads men to voluntary acknowledgment of the privilege of force and strength and thus makes them become a dust particle of that order which forms and shapes the entire universe.'† Indeed, it is a common factor of all authoritarian forms of thought that human destiny is directly controlled by sinister forces which cannot be fully comprehended by human reason or influenced by human action. The individual can thus only discover true happiness by subordinating the will to the dictates of these higher powers. Such is the nature of fascist 'idealism' to which such frequent and raucous appeals were made. This idealism is false, however, for true idealism must be an affirmation of the self, it must be the expression of the hope and the desire for the development of individual freedom. Thus for Fromm the only antidote to fascism is the unfolding of the free, critical and spontaneous individual, which is only possible within the framework of a democratic socialist state.

Fromm's work is an imaginative application of the psychology of Karen Horney and the philosophy of the young Marx to the problem of the personal basis of fascism. As such it offers helpful insights into the subjective moment within fascist mass movement, but it does not offer a satisfactory explanation of fascism itself. From Fromm's analysis it is possible to see how the reserve army of fascism is formed, but not how it is set in motion. Fromm was the first to admit this limitation, for if social character results from the dynamic adaptation of human nature to the structure of society, then clearly the structural economic causes cannot simply be ignored, and Fromm's historical data are all too often sketchy and dubious. Moreover, if bourgeois society has created the social-psychological and ethical preconditions for fascism, it is difficult to see how, in Fromm's terms, it can also provide the context for the development of a socialist humanism in which the art of loving can be developed, and Fromm's insistence on the power of individual choice is hardly a satisfactory solution to this problem. Thus by deliberately concentrating on the psychology of the individual Fromm makes it difficult to

* In *Faith for Living* (New York, 1940).

† *Mein Kampf* (New York, 1940) p. 411.

discover the objective social roots of fascism.

Most psychologists, however, felt that Lasswell, Reich and Fromm were placing too much emphasis on social forces and were thus deviating from psycho-analytical orthodoxy. A counter-attack was mounted by those who insisted that the key to fascism lay in the character structures of the fascist leaders. Although Mussolini's posturings and rumoured sexual appetite excited some comment, it was Hitler who was the most favoured object of such speculations. Thus Raymond de Saussure told the scientific world in 1942 of Hitler's carpet-biting and curtain-climbing, and his inability to achieve orgasm except by means of complicated and obscene mental presentations. He claimed that Hitler suffered from an Oedipus complex, paranoia and strong homosexual tendencies coupled with a castration complex, a narcissistic desire to dominate and the need to channel his sexual energies so as to hide his impotence from the public. The Führer was only able to overcome this impotence with Jewish women and, for reasons which remain equally obscure, with Frau Goebbels and Frau Göring.

As Saussure completed his psycho-portrait of this madman he began to ask himself why he had become the leader of a great nation. It was clear to him that 'the Reich is for him [Hitler] a force that replaces the phallic force of a normal man', but the question still remained why the German nation was such a willing tool. His answer was similar to that of many other psychologists. German fathers were authoritarian thus giving their sons marked homosexual characteristics, making the 'fatherland' into an idealistic mother – a curious form of transvestism – and this leads to servility towards the collective. This was combined with the congenital Prussian love of violence, war and cruelty. The overdeveloped German super-ego, the product of the authoritarian family, was partially replaced by a secondary super-ego formed during the First World War. This dualism led to a disintegration of the personality which was exploited by men like Hitler, who enabled many lost souls to find a place for themselves in his new paranoid society.

In 1942 Erik Erikson claimed that fascism was a form of adolescent rebellion which Hitler, with his pronounced rejection of his father and ambivalent attitude towards his mother, was uniquely able to exploit. The 'tune of the Pied Piper' had such tremendous appeal because it awoke 'archaic and infantile residues' within German society which Hitler, because of his particular psychological development, could so easily articulate and manipulate.

Such attempts to explain fascism in terms of psychologistic person-alism merely serve to obscure the true roots of fascism and make it diffi-cult to learn anything from the experiences of the past. Although most of the material on which the various diagnoses of Hitler's psychosis are based has subsequently been proved to be utterly false, it still remains true that his life provides ample material for psychological speculation, but such musings should not be confused with an attempt to explain fas-cism. Such an attitude is of course heresy to strict psycho-analysts. Otto Fenichel, for example, was accused of 'betraying psycho-analysis' when he correctly suggested in 1940 that anti-semitism was caused in part by forces which were external to the personality. The insistence by many psychologists that fascism is in the mind, and that its social manifestations are the articulation of psychological drives, is a dangerously misleading and reactionary view which makes it impossible either to understand a social movement like fascism, or to develop psychological techniques in the social sciences.

Individual psychology based on exceedingly dubious evidence is liable to produce some peculiar results, and there are many painful instances in the literature of the time of such bizarre and fanciful speculation masque-rading as science. Mass psychology seemed to offer some scope, and it further strengthened the widely held belief that fascism was the direct re-sult of a mass movement, and that it was the masses rather than the social system who were to blame for fascism. Thus even in the work of Reich and Fromm there is a tendency to use political economy merely to find the origins of the fascistic personality rather than the origins of fascism itself. Capitalism, it is argued, tends to foster the authoritarian person-ality structure, and thus social psychology provides the groundwork for the theory of totalitarianism. The link between psychological theory and the theory of totalitarianism can be most clearly seen in the work of Hannah Arendt, a scholar who owes a considerable intellectual debt to the Frankfurt School of Critical Theory, where many of the psycho-logical theories were developed.

Since 1895, when le Bon published his *Psychologie des foules*, the term 'masses' had had a largely negative connotation, a view which was further confirmed by the influential works of Spengler and Ortega y Gasset. As far as theories of fascism are concerned these ideas find a cer-tain resonance in the work of such scholars as William Kornhauser, Sig-mund Neumann, Talcott Parsons and Hannah Arendt, aspects of whose work are discussed later in this book, but for social psychologists who

approached the problem of fascism in this manner the more trivial literature on the subject had a greater appeal. One of the first such books to
appear was published in 1919, thus before the rise of fascism, and was to
have considerable influence on writers on the psychology of fascism as
well as the general reading public. W. Trotter's *Instincts of the Herd in
Peace and War* is a loosely argued and often very silly book, but it
preached a simple message which had an immediate appeal. Gregarious-
ness is a primitive and fundamental quality in man. It is the desire for
oneness which holds the pack together, and thus it is those who are essentially unstable and who refuse to belong that are most likely to become
leaders. For Trotter there are three basic forms of herd instinct – 'the
wolf is united for attack, the sheep is united for defence, but the bee is
united for all the activities and feelings of its life'. The Germans form a
'lupine society' which the English as bees find hard to understand. The
only way to control wolves, like dogs, is to give them a thoroughly good
thrashing, and the prevention of incipient lupine tendencies can only be
insured by the abolition of class divisions (though not by communism)
and by the establishment of a meritocracy.

Among the many books influenced by Trotter's ideas one of the more
interesting is Richard M. Brickner's *Is Germany Incurable?* published in
1943 and adorned by a highly laudatory introduction by Margaret
Mead. Brickner argued that the dominant psychological features of
German society were a strong feeling of hierarchy, lack of a sense of
humour, 'retrospective falsification' (the brooding over and falsification
of the past), a desire to find scapegoats, and a perverse internal logic to
the system. From this list he concluded that Germany was suffering from
national paranoia which enabled paranoids and latent paranoids to
dominate society and to impose their twisted world view on the normal
citizens who had escaped this 'paranoid contagion'. For Brickner Germany was sick, and had been sick for generations, and had to be set apart
as a special case among the nations of the world to be treated as a special
and highly dangerous patient.

The weaknesses of attempts such as these to explain away fascism by
regarding it as a symptom of a society that had gone mad are all too
obvious. Fromm's warning that a clear distinction between individual
and social psychology should be made was ignored. The historical data is
primitive and often wildly inaccurate. There is no discussion of the aetio-
logy of the disease. Most serious of all the impression is created that there
was no objective reason for fascist policies, and that it was all merely the

result of mental disturbance.

Along with the attempts to examine the psychology of fascism and even to explain fascism in purely psychological terms some psychologists tried to find ways of detecting fascist attitudes, so that measures could be taken against incipient fascism. The early work was concerned with finding adequate means of testing attitudes and of overcoming the problem that some people, even though they agree with a certain attitude, will disagree if it has the label 'fascist' attached. In 1943 A. H. Maslow attempted to list the basic components of the authoritarian character structure. These included a strong feeling of hierarchy, a drive for power, a hatred of some group (it did not matter much which), judgement of individuals by externals rather than internals, a single scale of values, a tendency to use people, sado-masochism, hostile attitudes towards women and a latent homosexuality, distrust of the intellect, refusal to accept responsibility for one's fate, and the search for security by compulsive routine and discipline. Maslow concluded that psychoanalysis could be used to cure such fascistic types, so that the analyst's couch could be used as a weapon in the war against fascism.

Much of this early work was crude in the extreme. Some articles came to the unexceptional conclusion that anti-semites were in fact anti-semites, and that fascists were fascists. An alarming degree of proto-fascism was discovered in the United States, where most of this work was done, and there was no evidence whatever that psycho-analysis could do anything to 'cure' fascists – there is not one instance of a potential or actual fascist being converted into a good liberal. Nevertheless the work went on and in 1950 T. W. Adorno and others published their classic book on the subject, *The Authoritarian Personality.**

For Adorno the anti-democrat is anti-semitic, ethnocentric, an economic conservative, holds rather rigid beliefs, condones violence against opponents, uses stereotypes, distinguishes sharply between 'in-group' and 'out-group' and admires strong men. The democrat by contrast is for the underdog, suspicious of patriotism, sympathetic to deviants, is in favour of science, and sees no great virtue in wealth. The conclusions of this study are certainly open to question. It is never clearly established whether there is a genuine syndrome of attitudes, or merely certain common elements in the two scales used for testing, some of which may be spurious because of the subjective assessments of the coders. For a proponent of critical theory Adorno allows an extraordinarily large norma-

* (New York, 1950).

tive element in the definitions of 'authoritarian' and 'liberal' which are not questioned and thus cannot serve the purpose of critical enlightenment. One critic has suggested that the right-wing attitudes are a set of progressivist clichés. There is also no attempt made to unmask left-wing authoritarians, not because they do not exist but because anyone, however authoritarian, who is on the left is bound to reject the slogans of the extreme right. Subsequent attempts to overcome this difficulty have not been successful. Another intractable problem with such an approach is the existence of rigid liberals who stubbornly exist in practice even though they are banned from the realm of theory.

Perhaps more serious are the questions of the social mechanisms behind the 'authoritarian personality'. The sociology of the study is weak, so that inadequate attention is paid to the social determinants of attitudes and the analysis of group membership and social status is often faulty. Even though many empirical studies show otherwise, the authors deny the class origins of ideology, which is seen as an expression of personality; indeed Adorno went so far as to argue that as fascists were recruited from all classes fascism had no specific class origin. Even temporary problems which face the individual, and which might have a significant effect on the response to particular questions, are ignored. There are too many broad generalisations which are often inadmissible. Thus hostility to one minority group may not necessarily be related to hostility towards another. Similarly it is not necessary to be an anti-semite to be an authoritarian. If situational factors are indeed important, then the 'F scale' is not much use as a predicter of future authoritarianism. The questionnaires used in the study to test attitudes are loaded to such an extent that 'authoritarians' are almost bound to emerge as anti-semites, and the 'irrationality' of a view is used to demonstrate that it must be due to personality factors. The process whereby childhood relationships to the father are correlated to prejudice is never explained, so there is no attempt to understand the dynamics of prejudice. Although it is asserted that the social structure merely sets off the chain of personality-impelled actions, the authors do not examine the way in which these attitudes become manifest in social groups and classes, and thus they are unable to show how political conduct follows from personality deformations and traits. *The Authoritarian Personality*, for all its importance in stressing the fact that fascism was not some historical mistake, and that fascist tendencies are immanent within modern society, fails to get to the real roots of the problem and does not provide a satisfactory non-subjective theory of the subject – fascism. The authors' rather naive belief in the ability of human reason to triumph over those economic and social forces which are, in their view, responsible for the maintenance of an essentially non-democratic status quo, does not inspire great confidence.

After the war the East German psychologist Dietfried Müller-Hegemann returned to themes which had been discussed by Fromm and Reich, in a book on the psychology of German fascists. Starting from Dimitroff's definition of fascism he tried, on the basis of an empirical study of a large number of individual fascists, to establish the relationship between social being and consciousness. The result was rather disappointing. His description of fascist personality types is, however, not without interest. He stressed the aggressive, sentimental, fearful and awkward behaviour of the typical fascist, his lack of will-power and his submissiveness to authority and lack of consciousness of personal social situations, yet at the same time his unthinking fearlessness when engaged in active struggle for the fascist cause, or when in battle. Müller-Hegemann also clearly demonstrated that acts of fascist terror and brutality created greater aggression and bound the fascists still closer to the fascist leadership. But this important point had been made many years before by Ernst Kriss, who saw complicity with crime as a basis of the fascist covenant, and was well summarised by the *Essener Nationalzeitung* in December 1942 when it wrote: 'In the eyes of international Jewry every German will be guilty.' For Müller-Hegemann the main principle of fascism is to suppress the aggressions of the subject, but also to use them for its own ends. The problem in this analysis begins when he tries to find the social origins of fascism and to integrate his findings into a Marxist-Leninist framework. On the one hand he falls back on a crude personalism, talking about the characters of Napoleon, Bismarck, William II and Hitler and ignoring the social roots of their psychological make-up and the social milieu in which such men were to have such influence. On the other hand he attributes the lack of social consciousness of the typical fascist simply to the capitalist mode of production and the alienation which this causes. Thus the Marxism in this work is not the methodological starting point, but rather a few slogans are tacked on to a piece of modest empirical research. This book seems to have confirmed many suspicions in the communist world that social psychology and psycho analysis was indeed irreconcilable with Marxism, and since 1955 no serious attempt has been made by a Marxist-Leninist to examine the psychology of fascism.

Although it was clear from these works that the most important aspect of a psychological investigation of fascism was the relationship between social being and consciousness, and although Fromm had made many helpful suggestions for further research, in the following years they were ignored in favour of a crude psycho-analytical approach which enjoyed a certain popularity, particularly in the United States, as the historical sciences looked for ways out of their methodological poverty. In 1962 Martin Wangh wrote an influential article on the psycho-analytical genesis of prejudice and Nazism. He argued that prejudice is always a retreat by the personality to a defensive position, that *Angst* triggers off a regression to a stage of early childhood. Nazism thus should not be seen as a result of the psychological problems of adults as such, but is due to problems of early childhood. 10 per cent of the voters in 1933 were small children in 1914, and the Nazi party was largely a party of youth. Therefore the experience of small children during the First World War was the key to an understanding of Nazism. Fathers were away in the war, mothers were deeply anxious. Childhood fears are projected on the mother, who now had to bear an additional burden, and the castration fears of the Oedipal phase became all the more acute. And as if things were not bad enough, the food shortages of 1917 caused oral regression which resulted in increasingly strong Oedipal tendencies, ego weakness, latent homosexuality and sadism.

Almost ten years later, in 1971, Peter Loewenberg published an article entitled 'The Psychohistorical Origins of the Nazi Youth Cohort' in the *American Historical Review* which popularised Wangh's ideas in the English-speaking world. Fascism was trivialised by being seen as a specifically generational problem. It was a regressive attempt to compensate for mothering and family life which had been inadequate. Weakened egos and super-egos turned readily to simple solutions. The active fascist youth 'reverted to phase-specific fixations in their child development marked by rage, sadism and defensive idealism of their absent parents, especially the father'. Such articles, by ignoring the social determinants of personality, marked a step backwards towards a reactionary psychologism and are almost of the same order of triviality as much of the literature published during the war on the perversions of the German mind. As Durkheim had insisted,* sociological phenomena cannot be explained by psychological means. Psychology is helpful in attempting to show what can be done to individuals and even groups under certain

* *The Rules of Sociological Method* (1895).

specific social conditions, and how objective social conflicts become sub-
jectivised. Without a clear understanding of these objective factors and a
theoretical mastery of them, psychology is functioning in a vacuum, and
is thus liable to yield such absurd, irrational and dangerous 'explanations'
of fascism.

These psychological theories and investigations are significant in that
they stress the importance of the subjective moment within fascism
which has often been denied, particularly by vulgar Marxists. The work
of men like Lasswell, Reich and Fromm contains many valuable insights
and suggestions for further enquiry, and as such it can hardly be even
compared to the wild speculations of the cranks and eccentrics of the
psycho-analytical school, even though the latter has had a considerable
and harmful influence. Psychology, when skilfully used, can help to
explain the mass movements behind fascism and may even illuminate the
psychological quirks of the fascist leaders, but it cannot explain what fascism is really about – its *cui bono*. The danger of this approach, however,
is to see fascism as an autonomous movement which transcends social
divisions, and which is to a certain extent antipathetic to capitalism. This
vital question is discussed at length in Chapter 5.

# Chapter 3

# The Theory of Totalitarianism

In the 1950s and the early 1960s the dominant theory of fascism in the western world was the theory of totalitarianism. The extraordinary popularity and the widespread acceptance of this approach is indication that it met an exceptional political need, and was used to legitimate certain political aims. The essential idea behind the theory of totalitarianism is that there is a vital structural similarity between communist and fascist systems which in turn form an antithesis to the western democratic system. The resulting theory, in its many variations, was thus able to provide a powerful ideological weapon in the Cold War.

The Third International, in its clumsy and dogmatic way, had always insisted on the close relationship between fascism and capitalism. Ample empirical evidence for this view was provided at the Nuremberg trials. The realisation that the only effective antidote to fascism was a thoroughgoing democratisation, which would include the extension of democracy to the work place, inspired the efforts of the German resistance movement around Stauffenberg and Moltke, and after the war the anti-fascist forces in both East and West Germany demanded democratic control over the economy and a restructuring of the relations of production. This view was held not only by the left but also by politicians as far to the right as Adenauer and Strauss. In Germany it seemed clear that the experience of fascism had discredited capitalism and that a genuine 'New Beginning' was not only possible but imperative if democracy were to survive and flourish.

These hopes were dashed in the Cold War. The struggle against the enemy of yesterday, fascism, was replaced by the struggle against an even more pernicious and insidious enemy, communism. The theory of totalitarianism performed the useful ideological function of equating fascism with communism so that the anti-fascist struggle could be converted into an anti-communist crusade. Capitalism, far from being the breeding ground of fascism, was seen as fundamentally opposed to totalitarianism and the best possible guarantee against unfreedom. Economists frantically sought to discover similarities between the socialist planned economy and the fascist corporate and war economies. The struggle against communism thus became an essential part of the effort to restore the market economy. The results were impressive. The demands for further democratisation were stopped, the western socialist parties were discredited and forced to rethink their programmes to meet the new mood, and the old elites and structures were restored. Anti-communism was thus far more than a protest against the barbarities and injustices of the Stalinist regime, it was the single most powerful weapon in the hands of the restorative forces who were determined to stop profound democratic changes which would destroy their privileged position. The theory of totalitarianism provided the scientific justification for this policy.

The theory of totalitarianism became so popular and was given so many different twists that it is extraordinarily difficult to deduce a common theory from its many manifestations. Indeed, Professor Fleron in his despair at the methodological sloppiness and dishonesty of many of the protagonists of the theory has remarked that it is little more than 'a "boo" label on a "boo" system of government'.* Such 'boo' systems include Sparta, India in the Mauryu dynasty, Ch'in China, the Empire of Diocletian and Calvin's Geneva. Definitions are equally vague: from the policy of economic planning and Popper's social engineering to Buchheim's colourful but ridiculous malapropism 'the creeping rape of man'. As the ideal type theories of totalitarianism ceased to have much in common with the current practice of totalitarian states, they were gradually abandoned in favour of a further proliferation of middle-range theo-

* 'Soviet Area Studies and the Social Sciences: Some Methodological Problems in Communist Studies', *Soviet Studies*, vol. XIX, no. 3 (1968) p. 339, n. 84.

ries until the theory became little more than a set of slogans. Rather than examining all the many variations of the theory, or attempting to systematise them, it is thus more helpful to examine the ideas of some of the most significant writers on totalitarianism.

For C. J. Friedrich totalitarianism is a new form of autocratic domination in modern industrial societies, which is historically unique and *sui generis*. It is distinguished from older forms of tyranny by the modern organisational forms and methods of social domination which enable total political control. In terms of structure, institutions and processes of law, fascist and communist regimes are basically alike. Totalitarian dictatorships are characterised by six basic features: (1) an elaborate ideology which covers all aspects of man's existence and which contains a powerful chiliastic moment; (2) a single mass party, led by one man, which forms the hard core of the regime and which is typically superior to, or intertwined with the governmental bureaucracy; (3) a system of terror by the party and secret police which is directed against real and imagined enemies of the regime; (4) a monopolistic control of the mass media; (5) a near monopoly of weapons; (6) the central control of the economy.

Friedrich's definition of totalitarianism has the great advantage of distinguishing totalitarianism from other early forms of dictatorship, so that the term does not lose all heuristic value by being applicable to an endless series of states of unfreedom. The last four characteristics depend in large part on the existence of a developed modern society with a high degree of technical proficiency which, when combined with a mass movement and a powerful ideology, give totalitarianism its specifically modern character. Totalitarianism is a 'perversion of democracy' in that the mass parties and the ideologies of these regimes are rooted in democratic systems, and their dictators proclaim that they are realising true democracy. The radical determination of totalitarian regimes to change society is in marked contrast to the essential conservatism of bourgeois democratic societies.

The six institutional and political similarities which Friedrich enumerated were soon seen to be inadequate. Changes within the Soviet Union in the post-Stalin era obliged him to modify the definition of totalitarianism in some significant ways so that he could still say 'boo' to the regime. It is not, however, the application of the theory to communist society that interests us here, but rather the adequacy of the theory as an explanation of fascism. A number of serious objections can be raised to the applicability of these criteria to fascist regimes. Ideology, by which Friedrich understands a 'reasonably coherent body of ideas concerning practical means of how to change and reform society, based on a more or less elaborate criticism of what is wrong with existent or antecedent society', played virtually no role in fascist regimes. Indeed it is difficult to establish the existence of any such ideology at all within fascist regimes, for the extraordinary collection of half-baked and cranky ideas certainly did not form a coherent whole.

This is of course not to deny that there was a fascist ideology, but it was an ideology of an altogether different order. Fascist movements were skilfully able to manipulate the frustrations of the masses in such a way that they did not threaten the basic structure of society. Social antagonisms were obfuscated and defused by the notion of community, in which rabid nationalism was but one constituent part, and existing class divisions were said to vanish as the nation stood together to achieve its destiny. The status quo was further reinforced by the leadership principle common to all fascist movements, which strengthened the authority of the family, the state and, in the economic sphere, the capitalists. Fascists also stressed the sinister threats to the regime by groups such as socialists, freemasons, Jesuits, homosexuals or any other group that could be identified as the enemy. The campaign against socialism, which culminated in the attack on the Soviet Union, combined this aspect of fascist ideology with its emphasis on the sacredness of private property which was part of the secret of its popular success. The scapegoat theory of the 'enemy within' reached its ultimate and most repulsive form in the extermination of the Jews. Lastly, there was a clear connection between fascism and militarism, which strengthened the authoritarian nature of the regime and served to prepare the nation for war. Fascists made no attempt to develop a coherent body of ideas. Hitler totally ignored the programme of the N.S.D.A.P., and indeed acted contrary to many of its points. Mussolini proclaimed 'our doctrine is action' and refused to be bound by any aim beyond the seizure of power. The fulminations of the S.S. ideologues were largely ignored, and Rosenberg's unreadable works remained unread. Fascism never produced anything remotely like the systematic body of ideas found in Marxism-Leninism. Its ideology served the destruction of the labour movement and of democracy, the strengthening of the position of the established elites, and the preparation for imperialist war. It did not provide a systematic critique of existing society, nor a guide to radical reform of the social structure. Thus fascist ideology is of a quite different order of things from communist ideology and hardly meets Friedrich's criterion in his first point.

Although mass parties were critically important for the success of fascist movements, and are one of the key factors which distinguish fascist regimes from other extremist right-wing forms of domination, the parties in fact played a subordinate role once the fascist regimes were established in power. In Germany the radicals in the N.S.D.A.P. who were demanding certain anti-monopolist and anti-capitalist measures were eliminated in the bloodbath of 30 July 1934. In Italy the experience was similar, though less drastic. Those within the fascist party who were demanding a 'second march on Rome' were not machine-gunned, as Mussolini had threatened, but expelled from the party. In both Germany and Italy the fascist party provided the mass base for a regime that was by no means always subservient to monopolists in the way that the Third International suggested. Although fascist regimes maintained the privileged economic and social positions of the capitalist elite, they determined the way in which this should be done, and, as Clara Zetkin had pointed out, their mass following greatly strengthened their political power. There is, however, a clear distinction between a mass following and a political party. As dynamic organisations with distinct political aims the fascist parties were destroyed, and became the tails that were often frantically wagged by the fascist dog. Although their importance to the regime should not be discounted in the manner of extreme heteronomic theories of fascism, they certainly did not play the role ascribed to them in Friedrich's theory of totalitarianism.

There can be little doubt that the use of terror was a characteristic of fascist regimes, and this aspect forms the basis of Hannah Arendt's theory of totalitarianism. The mass media were also subjected to close control. A near monopoly of weapons is a characteristic of most civilised modern states, and that this should be seen as typical of totalitarian regimes must be attributed to the American perspective. The logic of 'when guns are outlawed only outlaws have guns' is not very compelling to those who do not suffer from the frontier mentality. Lastly, the tendency towards a central control of the economy is a characteristic of most modern states as the problems of capitalist reproduction become increasingly difficult to master. It is for this reason that the theory of totalitarianism, having ceased to be useful for the understanding of fascist and communist regimes has formed the basis of other modish theories such as 'convergence theory' and the proclamation of the 'end of ideology'.

For Hannah Arendt totalitarian governments are distinguished from earlier tyrannies, despotism and dictatorships by a combination of permanent terror and ideological rigidity which rests not simply on the denial of all positive laws, even ones which they themselves have created, nor on the traditional lawlessness of early forms of despotic government, but, they claim, on direct obedience of the laws of history and nature from which all positive laws are supposed to spring. Thus, whereas old-fashioned tyranny could be seen as lawless and arbitrary in contrast to those states which upheld the rule of positive law, totalitarian regimes act according to a totally new understanding of the nature of law. Terror is thus rationalised to become the execution of apparently objective laws. It is not the brutality and bestiality of totalitarian regimes which is the essence of this terror, indeed to use her well-known phrase, evil can well be banal, but rather the total assault on human values and human freedom which it entails. Total terror aims at the destruction of the space between men. It does not just abolish freedoms and destroy liberties, it is a massive assault on man's very humanity. The psychological result of this on the individual is to leave him in a situation of total abandonment which is quite different from mere loneliness. Hannah Arendt's picture of totalitarianism is a moving denunciation of its vicious assault on individual dignity, but it is doubtful whether it is a particularly useful analytical tool, and it does not get at the heart of fascism. She is perfectly correct to stress the profoundly anti-humanist nature of fascism, and there can be no doubt that the way in which fascist regimes deny genuine humanistic and emancipatory movements is one of their most repulsive and dangerous features. Yet on the other hand her picture is perhaps over-pessimistic. More honest than most theorists of totalitarianism she admits that her definition can no longer apply to the Soviet Union, which she now refers to as a one-party state rather than as a totalitarian state. As far as the experience of fascist countries is concerned, the vast majority of the population was relatively unaffected by terror and the destruction of individualism. The level of vicious paranoia which characterised the Soviet Union at the height of the Stalinist purges was never attained. Terror was directed either at specific groups which enjoyed little sympathy from the mass of the population, or at opponents of the regime. Most Italians and Germans went about their daily life as they always had done, and regarded the government with a certain detachment. Those who were silently critical had moments of unease and foreboding but quietened their nagging doubts by the contemplation of the achievements of the regime.

Neither Friedrich nor Arendt address themselves to the important question of the aims to which terror was directed in totalitarian regimes. Few would deny that fascism and Stalinist communism employed a hitherto inconceivable degree of terror, but they employed it with quite different aims. Communist terror was directed towards a complete and radical change in society. Fascist terror reached its highest point with the destruction of the Jews. It made no attempt to alter human behaviour or build a genuinely new society. For all the horrors of the Gulag Archipelago nothing in Stalin's Russia remotely resembled the maniacal desire to destroy human life which, in its hideous bureaucratic form, was one of the most striking characteristics of German fascism.

Common to all theories of totalitarianism – whether it be the operational definition of Friedrich, the essentialist approach of Arendt, whether it be seen as a phenomenon of the twentieth century or yet another variation of an older form of tyranny, whether its intellectual roots go back to Plato as Popper argues, or to Voegelin's 'God-murderers', Marx and Nietzsche – is the insistence that the similarities between fascism and communism are greater than the differences. Western parliamentary democracy is then taken as the model 'open society' against which totalitarian regimes can be tested. It is, however, only when structures which limit and deform human growth, within both dictatorships and parliamentary democracies, are critically examined that a theory of totalitarianism can become objective and helpful. Yet so persistent is the belief in the essential similarity between fascism and communism that it is essential briefly to emphasise some of the fundamental differences between the two systems.

The most striking difference is socio-economic, and the value of an analysis which ignores the relations of production and the resulting social structure of the two systems is strictly limited. Whereas communist revolutions resulted in a radical change of the economic and political order, fascist regimes hardly touched the private ownership of the means of production and exchange, and by replacing the bourgeois state by the new fascist-leadership state this private ownership was indeed strengthened. Whereas the communists immediately set about the 'disappropriation of the disappropriators', the fascists established the same relationships in the economy as in politics with the introduction of the leadership principle to the workplace, which the flimsy ideology of the corporative state or the national-socialist revolution could not conceal. Even those state-planning organisations which have often been seen as the mark of the victory of politics over industry were dominated by the representatives of the monopolies, and their zigzag course was dictated as much by rivalries between the various sectors of industry as by changes in political direction, such as the determination to fight an imperialist war. Whereas the fascists talked at length about the destruction of old class barriers and the creation of a true national community, in fact the class divisions became even more pronounced and birth counted more than ever above ability as a means of social advancement. For all the talk of 'Hitler's social revolution' and the modernisation of Italy by fascism, the 'revolution' did nothing to redistribute property or to remove the barriers to social advancement; in fact it did quite the reverse. The revolution was aimed mainly at the destruction of most of the liberties and norms of the liberal state, and this led to the destruction of legal guarantees to the property of those who resisted the regime or who became the victims of racist purges. This violation of the bourgeois principle of property rights is obviously of a quite different order to the communist attack on the principle of private ownership of the means of production and exchange. Theft is always an affirmation of the principle of private property, never its denial. Whereas communist societies thus saw a radical restructuring of society, fascist regimes strengthened existing economic and social relationships and destroyed all progressive and emancipatory movements. The theory of totalitarianism in almost all its forms assumes that certain similarities in the exercise of power in communist and fascist states are more important than the far greater differences between their socio-economic structures and their political aims. The concept of totalitarianism lacks a concrete historical dimension and thus tends to become a seriously abstracted typology which mistakes certain appearances of similarity (which are often highly strained) for an essential identity.

The theory of totalitarianism was largely propounded by liberals who saw fascism and communism as massive attacks on the freedom of the individual, and by social democrats who had suffered the attacks of both the extreme right and the extreme left, but there is also a version of the theory which has been aptly described by Reinhard Kühnl as 'left-wing totalitarianism'. The best-known proponent of this view is Herbert Marcuse, who, like his associates in the Frankfurt School, attempted to uncover the roots of fascism in liberal society. Marcuse came to the conclusion that for all the marked differences between liberalism and fascism in their respective attitudes to the rights of man, individual freedom and democracy, both liberalism and fascism were based on the freedom of the economic subject to the full use of private property, and the state guaranteed this freedom. Liberal ideology is a highly flexible means of maintaining this unequal freedom, so flexible that it is even prepared to abandon its basic tenets at times of crisis. Faced with threats from the labour movement, liberalism is prepared to throw overboard its professed belief in democracy. In times of economic crisis it supports the interventionist state. The liberal belief in the inspired individual and the businessman of genius is a prefiguration of the fascist leader. Seen in these terms fascism is the appropriate theory and organisation of liberal bourgeois society in its monopoly capitalist phase when faced with a crisis situation. Marcuse has performed an important service in emphasising the roots of fascism within liberal society, but his approach is inadequate as a theory of fascism. Fascism was something rather more than a desperate attempt to maintain the capitalist mode of production and cannot be reduced to this simple definition. Furthermore, in Marcuse's view fascism is almost the inevitable result of monopoly capitalism, but this idea is belied by the historical facts. His theory thus cannot explain why fascism triumphed in Germany and Italy, but not in Britain, the United States or France.

After the defeat of fascism Marcuse developed his theory of 'one-dimensional' society, which became the ideological basis of much of the new-left activism of the 1960s. Modern liberal society, while maintaining the traditional liberties of bourgeois society, has in fact achieved, according to this theory, an unprecedented degree of conformism and control, so that far from being a haven of true freedom it is essentially totalitarian. The prisoner of one-dimensional society, unlike that of fascist society who is submitted to terror and brutality, is locked in a golden cage. The individual is trapped by a consumer society which can maintain a level of prosperity by vast armaments orders, keep a high degree of ideological control by various versions of anti-communism, and render innocuous any serious threat from the underprivileged by judicious welfare legislation. For all the apparent democracy of the system the individual has little control over decisions which affect his own vital interests. Modern man is a 'sublimated slave', but a slave none the less. The modern welfare state is 'an historical hybrid between organised capitalism and socialism, serfdom and freedom, totalitarianism and happiness'. Yet for Marcuse this tendency is not unique to capitalist societies. Socialist countries, although still retaining important differences, use many of the same techniques of control and manipulation, and both the Soviet Union and the United States are conservative class societies which are determined to crush all revolutionary movements which in any way challenge their power and authority.

Again there is much in Marcuse's work which offers valuable insights into modern society, but his tendency to make absolute and unhistorical statements is very pronounced. Recent years have witnessed such marked crises within capitalist societies that the stability of one-dimensional society has been severely challenged. With the crisis social movements have been set in motion which are less easy to control. The gilding on the cage is beginning to look a trifle tarnished. The contradictions within the system become all too evident, and the demand for radical change and for a more rational and equitable society becomes louder. The growing strength of opposition forces show that modern capitalist societies cannot simply be dismissed as totalitarian. Furthermore, by insisting on the totalitarian nature of modern capitalist society opposition groups all too often espouse a nihilistic, utopian and abstract policy which is doomed to failure. Marcuse, it must be added, has realised the shortcomings of his extreme version of one-dimensional society and has modified his views, not always to the taste of his more uncritical followers.

The most remarkable work which stresses the totalitarian nature of fascism is that of another scholar who was associated with the Frankfurt School, Franz Neumann. His masterly book, *Behemoth*, although inevitably in need of some revision in the light of more recent scholarship, remains one of the truly outstanding works on fascism and has lost none of its immediacy and flair since its publication in 1942. Neumann's starting point was the Frankfurt School's emphasis on the roots of fascism within liberal bourgeois society which faced a crisis situation politically, economically and socially. Fascism restored political stability by smashing the democratic opposition, the economic crisis was mastered by coercion and by rearmaments, and the social structure of domination secured by the destruction of the labour movement which threatened its economic base. Of all the theorists who can loosely be described as believing in the idea of totalitarianism, Neumann was the most insistent on the close connection between capitalism and fascism, and particularly between the big industrialists and the fascist leadership. Neumann also stressed the contradictions and rivalries between the fascist terror organisations and the traditional bureaucracy, army and police which largely adhered to the established norms of conduct and action, and which resulted in a state of organised anarchy and of 'divide and rule' which made organised opposition almost impossible. Neumann calls the resulting form of domination 'totalitarian monopoly capitalism'. His emphasis on the social roots of fascism and on its irrationality enabled him to avoid any facile identification of fascism and communism and accounts for the lasting value and importance of his work.

Thus, although the theories of totalitarianism have raised many important issues and set off a lively debate on the nature of fascism and communism, they have been far from satisfactory as theories of fascism. Only when the insistence on the essential identity of fascism and communism is denied is the theory capable of producing valid insights into the nature of fascism, but when this occurs 'totalitarianism' is given a different meaning and the original premises of the theory are abandoned. Liberal society is indeed challenged by the left and by the right, but the assumption that left and right must therefore be essentially similar is a severe hindrance to the understanding of either alternative.

# Chapter 4

# Ernst Nolte's Theory of Fascism

In the early 1960s it became increasingly clear that the theory of totalitarianism was no longer satisfactory. Significant changes in the communist world necessitated so many alterations in the criteria of totalitarianism that little was left of the original theory. Many theorists abandoned ship, others remained behind to patch up their leaking hulks. The time had come for a new theory of fascism in the western world. This task was performed by Ernst Nolte. His best-known book, *The Three Faces of Fascism*, was published in German in 1963 and met with widespread critical acclaim, not only for the contribution it made to the historical study of the Action Française, National Socialism and Italian fascism, but also for the novelty of his theoretical approach. Four further books appeared in the next five years which established his reputation as the leading western authority on fascism. Nolte's work is the longest and most detailed attempt to analyse the nature of fascism. It commands respect not only for its mammoth proportions but also for its enthusiastic reception by a large number of scholars of widely differing political views.

Nolte was well aware of the inadequacies of the theory of totalitarianism, and in an uncharacteristically witty remark he says that the theory of totalitarianism is a revenge for the theory of social fascism. He

also stresses that the Bolsheviks destroyed the preconditions of fascism – feudalism, the bourgeoisie, freedom of the press, patriotism and anti-semitism. But Nolte still leaves one foot firmly planted in the totalitarianists' camp. Rodzewski's famous letter to Stalin saying that Stalinism was Russian fascism without all the exaggerations of the western form, and without its illusions and mistakes, is quoted with warm approval. Like the theorists of totalitarianism he stresses the 'almost identical but typically modified methods' of fascism and communism, and even extends the theory by arguing that this applies not merely to the instrumentality of domination, but also to intentionality. Nolte's arguments to show this basic similarity of intention are opaque in the extreme. Thus Mussolini's histrionic agricultural policy, the *battaglia del grano*, is celebrated by Nolte as being essentially socialist with its 'eyes on the future, its irreverence for the past, and its concern with practical tasks' (*The Three Faces of Fascism*, p. 222), and it is compared to other great practical achievements such as his roadbuilding and housing programmes. In fact the *battaglia del grano* was an economic disaster which, far from modernising Italian agriculture, had the effect of strengthening a backward sector which was drastically in need of fundamental reform. The similarities between fascism and communism, for Nolte, are that both are social revolutionary movements. All the sociological and historical evidence which shows that the fascist regimes in practice were not in the least bit concerned with any kind of social revolution, and were in fact the most determined opponents of any such movement even within their own parties, is largely ignored. In his search for similarities Nolte came up with some extraordinary ideas. The fascist attack on the Soviet Union was a 'triumph of that international element which, from the very beginning was at least partially present in all kinds of fascism and which was a part, a mirror image and a counterpart to Marxist internationalism'.*
Equally absurd is the notion that the idea of race plays the same role in fascist ideology as the proletariat does in Marxism. We are asked to believe that the 'basic structure of its (fascist) practice' was socialist in character. Fascism in Italy was a development dictatorship, as was Stalin's regime in Russia – though we are never told why Italy resolutely refused to develop. Similarly, Hitler is seen as something of a socialist because if he had wanted to nationalise German industry he probably would have done so. From Hannah Arendt Nolte takes the definition of totalitarianism as total terror – that quantitative point in the application of terror

* *Die Krise des Liberalen Systems und die faschistischen Bewegungen* (Munich, 1968) p. 172.

when a change of quality takes place. For Nolte this stage was not reached until the assassination attempt on Hitler on 20 July 1944 when the power of the army to act as a conservative brake on fascist excesses was finally broken. Such a view is based on a lack of understanding of the role of the army in Nazi Germany and an exaggeration of the differences between Hitler and his generals.

Part of the problem lies in the fact that Nolte rejects the theory of totalitarianism on the grounds that it is an ideal type theory which also fails to stress differences between communism and fascism. Few versions of the theory of totalitarianism are in fact strict ideal type theories, and C. J. Friedrich is careful to reject ideal types in favour of a theory which defines the phenomenon by a description of its operational parts. Similarly, few theorists would argue that there was a complete identity between fascism and communism, although, as has been shown, the main stress of the theory was on similarities rather than differences, which were always regarded as secondary. A misunderstanding of the theory of totalitarianism, coupled with a considerable attraction to it, makes much of Nolte's writing singularly difficult to unravel.

Like the earlier theorists of totalitarianism, Nolte concentrates on the political, organisational and ideological structure of fascism, but overlooks its functionality – precisely that aspect of fascism which is of the greatest importance to Marxist writers. Whereas the theorists of the Frankfurt School argued that the roots of fascism were deeply imbedded in liberal bourgeois society, Nolte sees fascism arising from the failures and weaknesses of liberalism, from the 'crisis of the liberal system'. For Nolte liberal society is a pluralist system of give and take, or as he puts it: 'liberal society is a society of abundance – all forms of theoretical transcendence can develop independently, although not without being affected externally; a self-critical society – the attainment of practical transcendence remains subject to criticism; an uncertain society – it is continually subject to self doubts'.* Or in another passage: 'Bourgeois society is that form of society in which the leading class performs its task of establishing the technical and economic unity of the world, and emancipating all men for participation in this undertaking, in ever new political and intellectual compromises with the hitherto ruling powers: it is the society of synthesis.'†

For Nolte the constitutive factor in bourgeois society is this element of

* *The Three Faces of Fascism*, p. 451.
† Ibid.

ideological compromise within a self-critical but all-embracing ideology of the 'unity of the world'. The essential components of its ideology are personal freedom and liberty of conscience, freedom of speech and of the press, the protection of the relatively free working of society and the rejection of the interventionist state. For all Nolte's talk about the society of synthesis and the pluralism of the system, within liberal society there are profound contradictions, of which the most obvious is that between capital and labour. Liberal ideology and the interpretation of it by Nolte serve to disguise this fact, and a theory of fascism which is based on a faulty understanding of liberal society, which mistakes the appearance for the reality, the ideological form for the true basis, and which ignores the historical dimension of that society, cannot be successful in uncovering its true nature. Fascism cannot be understood in terms of a phenomenology of ideological formations, but only in terms of its fundamental objective causes. The roots of fascism, like those of any other social movement, are not in the mind or the realm of ideology but in society.

In his preliminary definition of fascism Nolte describes it as 'anti-Marxism which seeks to destroy the enemy by the evolvement of a radically opposed and yet related ideology and by the use of almost identical yet typically modified methods, always, however, within the unyielding framework of national self-assertion and autonomy'. By insisting that the anti-socialist thrust of fascism is a more fundamental criterion of fascism than anti-parliamentarianism or anti-semitism Nolte was making a step away from the theory of totalitarianism, but at the same time by stressing the 'almost identical methods' he did not burn all his boats. This definition of fascism is based on organisational practices and outward manifestations, the objective structural roots of ideological formations are ignored. This enables Nolte to develop a typology of what he calls the 'inner-political level' of fascism. The scale begins with 'pre-fascism' (the Pilsudski regime) and moves through 'early fascism' (Action Française) to 'normal fascism' (Italy) and finally 'radical fascism' (national socialism).

The inner-political level is based on a comparison between the fascist parties and other political movements and is revealed in the daily struggles of the political parties. The motivating force behind the inner-political is the political. It is here that Nolte applies his 'phenomenological analysis' in the hope of situating fascism within a schema of the history of ideas and to allow the phenomenon to reveal itself in terms of its own political practice.

Nolte's use of the term 'phenomenological' is somewhat perplexing. At the beginning of *The Three Faces of Fascism* he rejects historiography and typology (only to go ahead and use both) in favour of allowing the phenomenon to 'speak for itself' without imposing any extraneous definition upon it. A phenomenon is a social fact which is conscious of itself – in other words, it has an ideology. Phenomenology, for Nolte, is an understanding of these phenomena as they present themselves in their own terms. His method thus does not involve criticism from outside, nor is it mere description.

Although the term 'phenomenology' is not subject to precise definition, it is difficult to see quite what this enterprise has to do with what is commonly regarded as phenomenology. Although Nolte was a pupil of Heidegger, there is nothing here of the master's phenomenological ontology, and we are spared from any fireworks' display of the ontological and the ontic. Nor does he take into account Husserl's insistence on viewing the subjectivity of consciousness in relation to the objective basis of intentionality. In fact Nolte's approach has little to do with phenomenology. The idea that things should be seen as they show themselves to be, that meaning must be found within the phenomenon rather than forced upon it from outside, is a fundamental contention of hermeneutics. This in turn became the basis of historicism. Problems of the causality of historical events are ignored, and historical phenomena are examined in isolation. The result is an ahistorical and undynamic relativism which ignores the social dynamics of fascism. Nolte's 'phenomenology' is thus little more than historicism in fancy dress.

A major problem with such a methodology is that it is likely to view a social phenomenon such as fascism as dead and gone, or as Meinecke would put, as a 'transient moment in the endless movement of becoming'. After fascism was defeated in 1945 it ceased to be, in Nolte's terms, a world historical phenomenon. As it is no longer a phenomenon it cannot be the object of study by Nolte's phenomenological method. Fascism is thus dead, not because it has ceased to exist, but because Nolte's method is incapable of dealing with it. Fascism is identical with its historical form, therefore it belongs to the past. This must surely be one of the most remarkable confessions of methodological inadequacy. In a later book he tried to correct this obvious weakness by claiming that fascism could occur in the United States if there was a regime which emulated those of Hitler and Mussolini. But this tautology is hardly helpful, and a theory of fascism which concentrates on the political, organisational and ideological structure of fascism and which ignores or even denies its functionality, is incapable of being used to analyse fascist tendencies in the modern world, and is thus severely limited.

The political level of fascism is the object of his phenomenological analysis. Through the fascist rigmarole the relations between the immanent and the conscious are supposed to be revealed. At the political level fascism is the 'life and death struggle of the sovereign, martial, inwardly antagonistic group'. For Nolte all known societies are characterised by their determination to preserve their sovereignty, their willingness to fight and their inward antagonisms. Hence the appeal of the vision of a society that is universal, peaceful and inwardly harmonious: in other words, a socialist society. In the struggle between these two world views fascism is the most extreme form of the traditional social mode. Thus Nolte is able to fit fascism into a schema of history and at the same time emphasise its anti-socialist thrust. Radical fascism is thus the most striking condemnation of class society in that it discredits the ideas of nationalism, war and class. However, these considerations are examined at such a level of abstraction that it would be a mistake to assume that Nolte is here making a plea for socialism, and in spite of this clear admission that all is not well with the 'society of synthesis' he soon recovers his liberal composure.

Nolte's theory of fascism is a triple-deckered affair. The third level is even more rarefied; it is the metapolitical level. This philosophical approach to fascism, in which Nolte, for all his philosophical training, is at his most obscure and confused, reveals that fascism is 'resistance to practical transcendence and the struggle against theoretical transcendence'. Nolte does not give us any satisfactory definition of what he means by transcendence. He does not imply Aquinas's religious usage, nor Kant's critical meaning, nor even Heidegger's existentialist definition. Stripped of much of the jargon transcendence here means little more than going beyond the immediately given. In Nolte's language transcendence is the 'fundamental capacity for distinguishing between being and that which is, between God and world, between "ought" and "is"'. Practical transcendence is 'the social process, even in its early stages, which continually widens human relationships, thereby rendering them in general more subtle and more abstract – the process which disengages the individual from traditional ties and increases the power of the group until it finally assails even the primordial forces of nature and history'. Theoretical transcendence is the 'reaching out of the mind beyond what exists and what can exist toward an absolute whole'.

This all sounds most impressive, and indeed theoretical and practical transcendence are elevated to become the fundamental human attributes. But when these definitions are operationalised and applied to the real world the result is disappointingly banal. 'Practical transcendence' means very little more than the idea of progress. This enables Nolte to say a few kind words about Marx and Lenin, who, unlike the fascists, were on the side of practical transcendence. This earns Nolte a stern rebuke from C. J. Friedrich for making such a distinction between fascists and communists, but it also leads to further confusion in Nolte's own argument. For all the rigmarole about traditional values and the cultural pessimism of fascist movements they had always supported industrial expansion and modernisation. Indeed Nolte goes further than the evidence will allow in stressing the practical modernising role of fascist regimes which, as we have seen, he compares to socialist efforts in the same field. Fascism, for Nolte, is thus a 'development dictatorship' and it is difficult to see how this can be construed as a denial of practical transcendence. A further problem is that Nolte has to insist that Marxist practical transcendence is aimed against theoretical transcendence in that the genuine universality of post-revolutionary society makes it no longer necessary for the individual to affirm himself by theoretical transcendence. To drive the point home that there is a clear distinction between the liberal and humanist affirmation of transcendence and Marxism, this extraordinary idea is made out to be the central concept of Marx's thought.

The confusion over practical transcendence is further compounded in the discussion of theoretical transcendence. Although fascism clearly perceived itself as a doctrine of salvation, Nolte insists that this must be seen as mistaken. Doctrines of salvation are transcendental, but fascism is anti-transcendental, therefore it cannot be a doctrine of salvation. Fascism in other words cannot have an ideology, because ideologies presuppose the universal nature of man, which in turn necessitates theoretical transcendence. If we are to accept Nolte's rather bizarre definition of ideology then his entire effort to examine the phenomenology of fascism was wasted. Phenomena are phenomena because they express themselves in ideologies. We are now told that fascism has no ideology because it is opposed to transcendence. Therefore there is nothing for Nolte to study, and fascism is as immune to his analysis as a steel mill or a slag heap. As

Helmut Kuhn has pointed out, Nolte asks us to see the essence of fascism as the 'enthusiastic negation of the source of all enthusiasm, a battle of annihilation against transcendence which is set in motion by transcendence itself'. It is difficult to see how this circular argument can be of much help to an understanding of fascism.

In order for him to show that there is a transcendental moment in fascism, Nolte refers to it as an 'anti-Christian catholicism'. Although this phrase is largely meaningless, it is useful for Nolte's purpose in that it makes it impossible for a believing catholic to be a fascist. Faced with the embarrassing fact that a large number of catholics were indeed fascists Nolte smugly insists that they could not really have been catholics. There can thus be no such thing as 'clerical fascism', only 'clerical pseudo-fascism'.

Thus at the metapolitical level all that can give fascism its dynamic is *Angst*, a powerful weapon borrowed from Heidegger's philosophical arsenal. Of course this is not merely ordinary fear, but fear of transcendence, a fear which, in German fascism, is directed against the Jews, who are a kind of symbolic representation of the historical process itself. The understanding of this fear enables Nolte to extend towards fascism that degree of 'sympathy' which the historicist enterprise demands – the sympathy of the psychologist for the pathological. But this does not get us very far, for the really interesting relationship between *Angst* and prejudice is never examined. Fear in Nolte's scheme of things is a metaphysical concept that seems to be far remote from society, so that the social roots of racism are ignored, and anti-semitism becomes the *deus ex machina* which enables Nolte to continue with his enquiry.

For all his talk about a 'non-partisan' theory of fascism, by which Nolte means a politically independent approach, his discussion of transcendence reveals his political stance. Fascism is inhuman because it denies both practical and theoretical transcendence. Communism is partially inhuman because it denies theoretical transcendence, and conservatism because it denies practical transcendence. Only liberal-bourgeois society is able to realise the full human potential. By discussing fascism in this manner and at such a level of abstraction the social origins of fascist movements are either ignored or dismissed as irrelevant, and the vital questions of the functionality of social movements are omitted. Since Nolte rejects all heteronomic theories of fascism which stress the common interests of different groups, or see fascist movements as the marionettes of powerful sectional interests, he is scornful of sociological approaches to fascism. For him the inadequacy of sociological theory is amply demonstrated by the fact that social groups do not act as a whole. Thus to say that the bourgeoisie supported fascism is merely banal, it does not explain why many bourgeois did not follow the fascists. He correctly stresses the difference between fascism and other forms of ultra-conservative or military dictatorships. He sees fascism as a phenomenon of advanced industrial society. He concedes the non-identical identity between fascism and the bourgeoisie, but hastens to insist that the socialist origins of fascist thought made the fascist movement relatively independent from the bourgeoisie. In order to establish this dubious idea, a man like Mussolini has to be elevated to the rank of a major thinker, indeed he is all too prone to mistake the fulminations of any third-rate ideologue for philosophy. The massive sociological evidence which shows that fascism was not a social-revolutionary movement is ignored or dismissed, because Nolte has made his mind up that at the philosophical level it has to be, even if in real life it was not. The lack of sociological understanding in his work is best demonstrated by his joke that if the mass support for national socialism came from the petit bourgeoisie, the same is true for the Salvation Army.

Fascism, in this theory, is made to exist outside its social determinants. For Nolte sociology is only capable of saying something about the social structure of the country in which fascism triumphed, it is not capable of making any meaningful statements on the fascist movements themselves. Fascism is thus located in the mind, expressing itself in its parades and uniforms and in its mass rallies. Thus the best example of Nolte's approach is his picture book on fascism, which shows us nothing but photographs of the Pied Pipers and their uniformed followers.* Nolte's obsession with outward appearance, rather than the sociologists' concern with social background, led him to produce a dangerously trivial book.

The question remains why a theory of fascism which is both limited and confusing should have been so widely accepted and received such critical acclaim. It is partly because Nolte has moved away from the theory of totalitarianism, although not quite as far as it might at first seem, but has not abandoned the anti-communist stance of the earlier theory. Seen in these terms he has successfully revised the theory of totalitarianism to meet the ideological exigencies of a changed world. He has also attempted to free man from the burden of the past by insisting on the epochal nature of fascism; but this in turn is dangerous and misleading

* *Der Faschismus von Mussolini zu Hitler* (Munich, 1968).

for it blinds men to the dangers of fascist tendencies in the present. A genuinely scientific theory of fascism must examine the historical form in terms of later developments, so that fascist tendencies in present-day society can be uncovered. Such a theory not only illuminates the past, it also acts as a guide to action. It recognises that fascism can be stopped, and that the present can be transformed so that man may be emancipated. It can illuminate the possibilities and the limitations of human practice. Nolte, by looking at fascism from outside, has failed either to illuminate the past or to provide a guide to the present.

# Chapter 5

# Fascism and Industry

Central to all socialist theories of fascism is the insistence on the close relationship between fascism and industry. Conversely the main thrust of the attack on socialist theories has been to deny this relationship. The situation is made even more confusing by the fact that within the socialist camp there are wide differences of emphasis between those who stress the theoretical aspects of fascism, and those who are loath to move more than a few steps away from empiricism by making a few pious quotations from *Das Kapital* and who argue that too much theory has a disastrous effect on political practice. The delicate balance between theory and empiricism is all too easily tipped in the direction of empty theorising or the uncritical and unsorted compilation of facts.

Part of the problem results from drawing an inadmissible distinction between 'politics' and 'industry' which has resulted in lengthy, and largely fruitless debates on which enjoyed primacy. If politics and industry are seen as moments of a capitalism which, in both Germany and Italy, was marked by a high degree of state intervention, even before the time of fascism, then this duality largely disappears. Within this system heavy industry was favoured, the labour movement dragooned and increased profits achieved. This was only possible because of the co-operation between the fascists and the industrialists. The fascists destroyed the labour movement, actively helped the further exploitation of labour, pursued an aggressive trading policy, worked for autarchy, gave the order for massive re-armament, and finally unleashed a world war. All this enabled heavy industry to achieve maximum production at minimum cost, and thus ensured vast profits. In return for these rich rewards the industrialists were content to leave the political leadership of the country to the fascist elite. As Franz Neumann pointed out, German big industry had never liked democracy, the labour movement, civil rights and freedoms and was delighted to use the fascists to destroy them. Conversely the fascists welcomed the aggressiveness and the entrepreneurial skills of German industry and used them to stabilise their own authority. Fascism and big business thus had essentially identical interests. The fascists consolidated and increased their power. Industry extracted additional profits. One hand washed the other.

Seen in these terms fascism is characterised by the use of terror in order to stabilise the capitalist mode of production in which there is a mutual interdependence between the functional capitalist elite, not only in the economic sphere, but also in the bureaucracy and the military, and the fascist executive authority which is no longer bound by the political restraints of the bourgeois liberal state, and which is determined to continue the interventionalist policies of the capitalist state and to increase them to the point that the maximum realisation of absolute surplus value is achieved – in other words the highest possible degree of the exploitation of labour. Jürgen Kuczynski sees in this system a reversion to barbarism, and indeed the use of open terror in order to achieve the production of absolute surplus value is reminiscent of the economic practices of the period of primitive accumulation, in which terror is used as an economic force. This system is clearly in marked contrast to the modern capitalist state in which the production of relative surplus value is conducted within the framework of a welfare economy. In economic terms fascism was the creation of an exceptional capitalist state, exceptional in that it was only possible with a degree of deficit budgeting, hyperinflation, reduction of living standards, regimentation of labour, executive violence and outward and inward aggressiveness which would be intolerable to the normally functioning liberal state.

This approach, which stresses the dialectical relationship between the capitalist functional elite and the fascists, must be clearly distinguished from the heteronomic theory of the Third International, which saw the fascist party as mere agents of monopoly capitalism. The extraordinary determination of Marxist-Leninists to preserve this theory in its pristine form deserves comment. Although crude and undialectical it serves a useful ideological function. Fascism was the result of the sinister machinations of the monopolists, therefore the communist parties were in no sense responsible for the victory of fascism. There were voices within the International, among them Zinoviev, Clara Zetkin, Gramsci and Togliatti, who warned that fascism could only succeed if the labour movement as a whole suffered a severe defeat, but the thesis that the defeat of the labour movement was one of the essential preconditions of fascism leads to a necessary self-criticism of the role of the communist parties and the communist International. Most communists, with the notable exception of some members of the Italian party, are unwilling to take this uncomfortable but essential step. Without such self-critical analysis of the role of the communist wing of the labour movement no fruitful strategy or tactics for the resistance of fascistoid tendencies in the present day by a broad labour front is possible.

The major fault of the traditional Marxist-Leninist approach is that it equates the machinations of groups of capitalists with the totality of capitalist society. Any theory which wishes to emphasise the relationship between fascism and capitalism must see capitalist society as a whole and must take this into account by looking at the complexities of the relationships between various strata of society. Such a theory must also analyse the economic problems of the society, rather than reduce them to a voluntaristic model whereby immensely complex relationships are seen to be 'one way' in that they are determined by a small capitalist clique. Even the most determined proponents of the Dimitroff thesis, the historians of the G.D.R., have been forced to admit that there are problems in applying the theory to the impressive mass of empirical data. Problems of the contradictions within fascist societies, and the relationship between the economic demands of the monopolies and the political trajectory of fascist regimes, can hardly be reduced to such a simple formula.

The economic system of fascism is therefore characterised neither by the 'primacy of politics', whereby the fascist regime exercised full political domination over the economy in a direct interventionist system, nor by the domination of the entire state by a group of monopoly capitalists. For all the close relationships between the fascist regimes and the capitalist elite, for which there is massive empirical evidence, and for all the similarities of the aims and intentions of both groups, and in spite of the fact that fascism was exceptionally useful for the capitalists, it would be a gross over-simplification to insist on an identity between capitalist elite and fascist party. The relationship is best described by the Hegelian concept of 'non-identical identity'.

Thus in Italy the industrialists wanted guarantees that wages would be kept low, the destruction of the organised labour movement, protective tariffs, and state guarantees against economic crises and unnecessary loss or risk. For all the talk of corporatism and the destruction of the plutocracy the fascists had abandoned their social reformist platform and were all too willing to oblige. The finance minister, De Stefani, pursued a conventional liberal economic policy, made possible in part by the beginning of a period of relative prosperity by 1925. The telephone, match-making and insurance industries were denationalised, along with a number of less important industries. There was a significant tax cut to encourage expansion, and the fascist demand for severe penalties on war profits was quickly forgotten. Government spending was drastically cut, and the budget balanced by an increase of indirect taxation. Inflation hurt the middle and lower classes and profited the industrialists and landowners. Massive assistance was given to industry and the banks by the extension of the powers of the C.S.V.I. (*Consorzio privato per sovvenzioni su valori industriali*). Whereas Mussolini announced that the economic policy of fascism was 'Manchester liberalism', there were those who were demanding autarchy, and protective tariffs particularly for grain and sugar. As it was, imports continued to rise causing a severe balance-of-payments problem and calls for a stabilisation of the currency. The regime destroyed the independent unions, ended the eight-hour day, forced wages down and increased per capita output. By these means labour costs were reduced by 30 per cent between 1927 and 1929. With the onset of the Depression wages were forced down still further. In spite of falling prices real wages dropped dramatically. In November 1925 the fascist Grand Council forbade all strikes.

In the early years of Italian fascism the industrialists and their interest group the *confindustria* were suspicious of the radical squadrist elements within the fascist movement and feared that the fascist unions were infected with revolutionary syndicalist ideas. By 1925 the squadrists and the *ras* were rendered innocuous. The fascist union boss, Rossoni, was dismissed, and Volpi di Misurata replaced De Stefani. The *confindustria* could now drop all its reservations about the fascists, and from then on the industrialists identified with the regime.

Volpi's first major act as finance minister was to impose a protective tariff on grain, and this initiated the beginning of a policy of direct state intervention in the economy. Along with this interventionist policy went the *leggi fascistissime*, the super-fascist laws, which further restricted the freedom of the working class and led to a regimentation of labour in the interests of the monopolies. The *battaglia del grano* was begun with much propagandistic rigmarole in order to help the balance of payments, and at the same time a massive foreign loan was used to try to stabilise the exchange rate in the battle for the *quota novanta* (ninety lire to the pound stirling, rather than the existing 154 to the pound). Although sectors of light industry objected to this policy on the grounds that it would make exports more difficult, the *confindustria* was delighted for it would destroy weaker companies, increase the trend towards monopolisation, lower import costs, lead to lower taxes, and could also be used to reduce wages still further. Rocco's law of 1926 destroyed such autonomy as remained even to the fascist unions, and in 1928 the *Confederazione Generale delle Corporazioni Fasciste* was disbanded. In April 1927 the *Carta del lavoro* was proclaimed which gave an ideological gloss to these measures. It made it quite clear that the intention of the regime was to control labour, but not industry, and asserted that the corporative state believed that private initiative was the only effective way to secure the maximum of production and that such initiative would be given full support by the state. State control over the work-force was further increased by the introduction of the work-book (*libretto*) in 1935, which controlled the movement of workers and registered their political activities.

With the beginning of the Depression these tendencies were further accentuated. Monopolies grew stronger by swallowing up the smaller firms. Banks rushed to the help of industry, and in turn had to rely on state financing to secure these loans. State intervention in the economy, which had already played an important role in fascist economic thought, was now further intensified. In 1933 the I.R.I. (*Istituto di Ricostruzione Industriale*) was formed. Based on the earlier I.M.I. (*Istituto Mobiliare Italiano*) it was designed to regulate and secure credit and to provide industry with the necessary capital which the three big banks, the *Banca Commerciale Italiana*, the *Credito Italiano* and the *Banco di Roma*, were no longer capable of providing in full. Thus the Depression marked the end of the old system of finance capital, and the big banks which were badly hit could no longer play the important role in control and supervision of industry which they, like the German banks on which they were modelled, had done since their foundation. The I.R.I. thus acted as an intermediary between the big banks and big industry and functioned as a kind of super-bank. Although this gave the state a high degree of control over the economy, the I.R.I. was all too willing to do the bidding of the monopolies, which were now guaranteed sufficient capital and were further aided by protective tariffs which excluded competitors. Gramsci wrote in his *Prison Notebooks** that fascist economic policy aimed to nationalise losses, but not profits. This is a perceptive remark, and it would be quite mistaken to believe that this state intervention resulted in either nationalisation or 'state capitalism'. Nor did it result in the modernisation of the economy, for in spite of the considerable extent of state control over the economy the state lacked the will and the determination to use that control to effect major changes. The I.R.I. helped private industry to overcome the Depression, speeded up the process of monopolisation and concentration, and although often exercising control it never altered the private nature of industry in any significant way. Thus 99 per cent of the coal, 80 per cent of iron, 65 per cent of steel, and 36·8 per cent of transport was controlled by the state, but the private form of these industries was maintained. The major difference was that the industrialists no longer had to rely on shareholders or financiers for capital, but got it through a state-controlled holding company. At a time of high risk and depression the capitalists were delighted to relinquish their nominal control in return for such favours.

The policy of autarchy was primarily designed to protect Italian industry from external competition, and was only secondarily aimed at preparation of the economy for war. The nationalist ideology of fascism in which this policy was dressed is a further example of the mystifying function of fascist ideology. The policy began with the *battaglia del grano* and the *quota novanta*, but it was not until the League of Nations' sanctions in 1935 against the Ethiopian campaign that the policy began in earnest. The instrument for this new policy was to be the corporations about which the fascists had spoken much but had done little. Twenty-two corporations were formed in 1934 for branches of industry and agriculture. At first they were merely consultative organisations, and in spite of the massive propaganda made on their behalf they had little real power. Such powers as they did have were of a regulatory nature, their policing functions made necessary by the effects of the Depression. The 'corporative state' never existed in fact, for there was no new economic

\* (London, 1971).

policy, no fundamental change in the structure of the economy, no major technical innovations, and no real authority to the *Consiglio delle Corporazioni* or to the minister of corporations. The corporations in practice helped big business and further reduced the element of competition within the economy. They remained subordinate to the traditional bureaucracy.

With the 11 per cent drop in the value of the lira in 1936 the policy of autarchy was further threatened, and coupled with the increased armaments programme triggered off by the Spanish Civil War these *dirigiste* policies were further intensified. In 1938 the *Comitato Corporativo Centrale* was formed with the active participation of representatives of big capital who served as experts. In 1939 the *Comitato Interministeriale per l'Autarchia* was tantamount to the creation of a war cabinet, for it was the highest decision-making body and executive branch of government. The final stage in the policy of autarchy was reached in 1940 with the resignation of Beneduce from the I.R.I., a man who had always been concerned to place the I.R.I. at the disposal of big business. I.R.I. was now in effect controlled by Bocciardo, the president of FINSIDER, the iron and steel section of the I.R.I. This change marks a distinct movement of emphasis towards heavy industry which was characteristic of the war years.

Few of these measures are uniquely fascist – they are typical of late capitalist societies. Many of the major organisations such as I.R.I., the *Confindustria* and the oil companies AGIP and ANIC which were combined to form E.N.I. (*Ente nazionale idrocarburi*) played an important part in post-fascist Italy. Indeed such an economy with a high degree of state intervention in the interests of private business is characteristic of most highly developed capitalist economies. What was unique to the fascist economy was the ferocity with which the labour movement was destroyed, the application of a wages and price policy which could not be softened by the action of the unions, and a policy of autarchy which, by cutting the country off from the world market as far as possible, made an aggressive imperialist foreign policy inevitable. The result was the creation of intolerable economic and social tensions which the regime was finally unable to contain. In 1943 the fascist regime was no longer of any use to the captains of industry, and indeed was little more than a hindrance to peace negotiations and a new phase of capitalist development. Fascism was destroyed, but fascism's major benefactors and beneficiaries survived.

Just as the Italian fascists owed their early successes to the active support of industry and landowners for their anti-socialist brutality and the 'March on Rome', so the Nazis owed their first major success at the polls in 1930 in no small part to the support of Thyssen and Kirdorf and to the sympathetic attitude of the Hugenberg press empire. Hitler's party offered the industrialists the destruction of the labour movement, decisive action to stimulate the economy, rearmaments and the creation of a strong and forceful 'national' government, a programme which was particularly appealing to heavy industry. The governments between 1930 and 1933 had failed to master the economic crisis, lacked the strength and support to order the economy, could not disregard the trade unions, and were unwilling to lower still further the living standards of the vast mass of the population. As the crisis deepened the remaining objections to a fascist solution to the economic problem were overcome, the more so because Hitler was careful to disassociate himself from his more radical 'left-wing' followers. Hitler told the industrialists that he would destroy democracy, the parties and the unions and unite the nation in a massive effort for economic and military reconstruction which was bound to profit industry. In a crisis situation industry and finance were prepared to support exceptional measures.

The German fascists promptly set to work. One of the very first measures after Hitler became chancellor was to disband the trades unions, crushing even the Nazi union organisation, the N.S.B.O. (*Nationalsozialistische Betriebszellenorganisation*) in 1934. The numerically strong N.S.B.O. was the organisational centre of the Nazi left wing, and its reorganisation under the D.A.F. (*Deutsche Arbeitsfront*) in January 1934 was part of the purge of the 'revolutionary' Nazis which was to reach its culmination in the 'Röhm putsch' a few months later. The working class thus had no organisational protection whatever against the employers, whose own power had been greatly increased. The D.A.F. was almost solely concerned with establishing what the Nazis called 'class peace' and ignored the fundamental interests of the workers. Thus freedom of the labour market, one of the basic freedoms of the liberal capitalist state, was abolished. All strikes were forbidden. Wage agreements could no longer be negotiated between workers and management. After the 'Leipzig agreement' of March 1935 the D.A.F. became largely concerned with fascist indoctrination, intensification of work and the enforcement of the wage freeze. This wage freeze had been announced in 1933 and remained in effect throughout the 'Third Reich'. Social-service benefits were also greatly reduced. As in Italy the workers were given work-books which recorded details of their activities and without which they could not be employed. Nazi wages policy made a sharp distinction between skilled and unskilled labour thus undermining class solidarity, and wages were based on output so as to exploit labour further. Hitler gave an admirable summary of national socialist wage policy when he announced that it was an 'iron principle of national socialism' that output should be increased but not hourly wages, although it must be admitted that like most fascist 'iron principles' it proved to be quite flexible when opportunist considerations dictated, so that a small sector of privileged workers did comparatively well under the Nazis.

One of the major pieces of legislation by the regime was the 'Law on the Ordering of National Labour' of January 1934. In this law the leadership principle (*Führerprinzip*) was applied to all aspects of employment. The employer was deemed to be a *Führer*, employees were followers (*Gefolgschaft*). Within industry the *Führerprinzip* was applied to the relationship between big and little firms, so the tendency towards further monopolisation and cartelisation was accentuated. Krupp as *Führer* of the association of German industrialists (*Reichsstand der Deutschen Industrie*) was able to exploit the new situation so as to favour heavy industry greatly and have a decisive voice in economic and social policy. Wilhelm Keppler, who played a vital role as intermediary between the fascist-party leadership and the captains of industry, was thus proved correct in insisting that the 'corporatism' propagated by some of the Nazi left wing was irreconcilable with fascist economic policy.

The tendency towards further monopolisation was also reinforced by two further pieces of fascist legislation: the cartel law of July 1933 and the stocks and shares law of 1937. The first law gave the cartels exceptional rights, even to the point of giving them semi-legal authority. Cartelisation became obligatory, all firms were obliged to join the appropriate cartel. The cartels could forbid the founding of new companies, and until the beginning of the four-year plan were able to fix prices. They were placed outside parliamentary control. The law governing shares gave exceptional powers to boards of directors and drastically reduced the influence of individual shareholders. This law reinforced the *Führerprinzip* in business and helped the aggressive capitalist managers such as Quandt and Flick to carve out even greater empires for themselves. It is partly responsible for the fact that between 1931 and 1938 the number of companies quoting shares was halved.

The national socialist profession to be the party of the 'little men' was soon proved to be false. Small businesses were often swallowed up by the larger concerns, or went into liquidation. In February and March 1939 two laws were passed which made possible the closing down of small and inefficient businesses – the revival of a practice during the First World War, and indicative that the economy was to be placed on a war footing. The same policy was also applied to wholesale and retail stores. All that remained of the 'anti-plutocratic' policy of the fascist regime was directed against Jewish property, so that the racist policy of the regime served the function of an *ersatz* anti-capitalism. But here again the profiteers were the Flicks and Wolffs and the Mannesmanns, not the 'little men'.

In the autumn of 1936 the four-year plan was announced, designed to maximise the efficiency of German industry and to force the rate of re-armament. The four-year plan office, with Göring as chairman, set about ending the market economy by taking over the price-fixing functions of the cartels, and by implementing a *dirigiste* command economy. The plan seemed to mark the end of private capitalism and the beginning of state capitalism, but in fact the plan helped a significant sector of big industry and speeded up the process whereby the larger companies grew at the expense of their weaker rivals. The 'price plenipotentiaries' of the four-year plan worked closely with the cartels, and were always considerate of the requirements of big industry. Planning within the four-year plan was largely the work of the big capitalists or their close allies, men like Karl Krauch and Karl Lange. It was not long before the cartels recovered the right to regulate prices. Thus, although the four-year plan marked a change of emphasis and tempo, and marked the hegemony of electrical and chemical industries, particularly I.G.-Farben, within the group of monopolies, it did not mark any radical departure in the structure and implementation of power over the economy. The monopolies retained the ability to dictate economic policy to a considerable extent, and to a degree that would have been impossible in the liberal democratic state.

Economic questions had always played a secondary role in national socialist ideology. Gottfried Feder's theory of interest slavery, which was attractive to petit bourgeois elements who felt threatened by the big corporations and banks, was a cunning method of standing socialism on its head. The existence of exploitation in society was thus explained not by class conflict but by racial conflict. In this theory it was not the possession of the means of production and exchange which was the source of power over others, it was the possession of money. Money in turn was controlled by modern banking systems, which were controlled by Jews. By controlling credit the Jews controlled the banks, the stock exchanges, industry and commerce. They interrupted the natural circulation of money in order to control the economy. Thus the way to free society from interest slavery was to destroy the Jews. Once the Jews were removed the economy would function naturally and racial unity would be restored to the state. The way would now be open for the creation of the 'national and social state'. The main aspects of the 'social' state were the right to demand unremunerated labour from its citizens, the right to increase taxation, and the right to print as much money as it wished. Thus a theory that had certain populist overtones could be used to justify the economic policy of the Third Reich, which so blatantly favoured big business. Feder also insisted that the major conflict in modern society was between sovereign states, rather than the socialist notion of a conflict between capital and labour. Thus the key to his system was vicious anti-semitism combined with an aggressive imperialism. This was the basis of all Nazi economic policy, and it had the advantage of being without any specific economic remedies, so that the regime could act in an entirely opportunistic fashion. Although Feder was only briefly employed in a leading position after 1933, his irrational ideas survived and continued to prove useful as a means of reconciling fascist theory with fascist reality.

The economic role of fascism in both Italy and Germany is thus clear. It helped to sustain and strengthen, and even to a certain extent transform, the capitalist system at a time when it faced a severe crisis. In this crisis situation capitalism also felt threatened by the labour movement, and restrained by bourgeois democratic control over the economy. Fascism crushed the labour movement and ended liberal democracy and with it the rule of law. With these restraints removed the capitalist elite was able to secure the depression of wages, the intensified exploitation of the working class, and greater profits. The fascist state set about deliberately stimulating production, but it did so in a way which particularly favoured big industry. Rather than massive expenditure on housing, education, medicine and recreation the regime concentrated on armaments, which guaranteed that profits would be high and the market could never be glutted because the appetite of the military for new weapons was insatiable. The 'little man' had to pay the price for huge state expenditure which only profited a small elite. Finally, fascist economic policy led to the military and political preparation for a major imperialist war. Thus both internally and externally capitalism reverted to a primitive brutality which characterises the ultimate form of the antagonistic society.

The close co-operation between big capital and the fascist regimes and their common roots in an antagonistic society should not be taken as a complete identity. The fascist parties assured the social position of the capitalist elite by destroying the labour movement and then the petit bourgeois anti-monopolists within their own ranks. But this did not mean that the fascists were merely the paid agents of the monopolies, or that they were content always to do the bidding of the capitalists. Thus in Germany the fascist regime would not accept the arguments of Thyssen and Schacht that an intensified armaments programme would be highly inflationary, would lead to an acute crisis in the foreign trade balance and result in a serious shortage of foreign currency. Hitler was determined that the armaments programme should go ahead, even at the cost of massive deficits and the collapse of the mark, for these effects could be undone by a successful war. He found willing support for this view from I.G.-Farben, A.E.G., Siemens and the Deutsche Bank, who all stood to profit from the autarchy policy and the huge investments for artificial oil and rubber. Heavy industry feared that they would have to make do with inferior domestic ores, and complained that exports would suffer, but once they supported the new policy they were given further help. Thus the *Reichswerke Hermann Göring* was formed to provide supplies of cheap domestic ore. A change had taken place whereby the leadership of Thyssen and Schacht was lost to I.G.-Farben and the Göring works, whose instrument was the four-year plan.

The change from Thyssen/Schacht to I.G.-Farben/Göring also marked a change in foreign policy. The heavy industrial grouping around Thyssen wanted a degree of co-operation with the United States and Britain so that Germany could become a powerful European power. By contrast the I.G.-Farben group saw in the Anglo-Saxon powers their major rivals and competitors and thus forced the autarchy policy and the preparations for war. In its extreme form the Marxist-Leninist theory insists that the radicalisation of German foreign policy after 1936 and the determined preparation for war were a direct result of the victory of the I.G.-Farben faction over the Thyssen group in an inter-monopolist rivalry. Conversely the supporters of the 'primacy of politics' insist that I.G.-Farben was able to oust Thyssen because of a major change in policy by the fascist leadership which no longer coincided with the interests of the Thyssen group. Neither of these arguments are compelling for the simple reason that they cannot be proved or disproved. All that can be clearly established is the similarity of aims between the fascists and the industrialists, a similarity which can be even more clearly demonstrated in the case of Italy, where the fascist party was less powerful than in Germany and thus did not have the same degree of independence.

Another version of the 'primacy of politics' is the argument that industry had to suffer from irrational fascist policies. Thus women were obliged to stay at home rather than work in the factories, their place being taken by unreliable prisoners of war and slave labour. A further example is that among the first Jews to be murdered were highly skilled armaments workers who were badly needed in industry. The problem with such arguments is that fascism is seen as irrational, industry as pragmatic, thus the anti-pragmatic is political and the triumph of the irrational is the primacy of politics. The destruction of the Jews may indeed have been irrational, but it was an integral part of German fascism, for racialism had a clear functional role within the system by providing a scapegoat for the problems of capitalism, socialism, democracy and war, and in turning men's minds away from the objective causes of these problems, and as such it has a certain functional rationality. By regarding fascism as irrational in this sense, or even worse by looking at it as a kind of madness, its true nature is concealed. The danger of looking at the relationship between politics and the economy in terms of rivalry, or of insisting on the primacy of either the political or the economic, is that the emphasis is being placed on a basic antagonism between the two when in fact it did not exist.

It is perfectly true that the industrialists were unwilling or unable to dictate policy to the fascist leadership, and it was not until the last stages of the war that they dared to refuse Hitler's orders when they ran counter to their own vital interests – such as the order to destroy all industrial plant lest it should fall into the hands of the Allies. Even the most assiduous of East German scholars have been unable to provide one single instance of German industrialists having a decisive effect on Nazi policy. But by contrast there is also no evidence of their refusal to accept the broad outlines of an economic policy which was greatly to their advantage. Industrialists were impatient at the regime's reluctance to introduce maximum wage rates, for the fascists still hoped to win the workers over to the regime. They would have preferred to have had German women rather than foreign slaves labour in their factories. They objected to the economic inefficiency of the mass murder of Jews. They were excluded from making those really important political decisions which affected the political course of the nation. They were plunged into a war which ended in defeat and destruction, and which made impossible demands on the German economy. But the industrialists were satisfied with the broad outlines of Nazi policy. They might have grumbled about slave labour but at least it was free; they profited both directly and indirectly from the destruction of the Jews, and they stood to reap vast benefits from a successful war. The industrialists did not submit themselves to Hitler because he was a madman who knew no restraint, they supported him precisely because although he played for high stakes he based his decisions on rational calculation. The economic situation of the country was critical, and they were prepared to risk a war which they could reasonably hope would be limited, in order that they might maximise profits. Only defeat convinced them that they were wrong. Thus, although they had to suffer interference which they sometimes found almost intolerable, and were horrified at the outcome of policies which they had initially supported, there was, in the final analysis, no profound conflict or difference between the aims and ambitions of the fascists and the industrialists.

Fascism was an attempt to overcome the antagonisms within modern bourgeois society made by the fascist party in close conjunction with the capitalist elite. The viciousness of the regime and its ultimate failure were not due to any rivalry between the partners. Indeed they remained together until the bitter end. Only in Italy, where the fascist system was less powerful than in Germany owing to the lower level of capitalist development, did the capitalists abandon the regime in a successful attempt to survive its collapse.

# Chapter 6

# Fascism and the Middle Classes

One of the earliest and most persistent theories of fascism is the 'middle-class theory', first put forward by Luigi Salvatorelli in 1923, developed and refined by sociologists, particularly in the United States, and now the most widely accepted autonomic theory of fascism. Briefly the theory is based on an examination of the social basis of the fascist mass movement from which the objective social function of fascism is deduced. By this means fascism is seen as an independent movement of the disgruntled middle and lower middle classes, and the close relationship between fascism and capitalism is denied.

One of the most distinguished protagonists of the middle-class theory of fascism is Talcott Parsons, who examined the social structure of western capitalist societies in order to find the roots of fascism, and then tried to find the reasons why fascism became a mass movement in Germany. Parsons used Durkheim's concept of 'anomie' in order to answer the first question, and argued that the internal tensions within capitalist society result in imperfect integration which can be so acute that the society begins to fall apart. This does not necessarily involve manifest social conflict, but rather a collapse of social norms which leaves individuals and groups without those fixed points of reference that they so desperately need. Generalised insecurity results in either a paralysis of the will and general inaction, or violent emotional excesses, fear and aggressiveness. The causes of anomie in modern society include the Industrial Revolution and rapid technological change, the movement of population from the countryside to the towns, relative social and professional mobility, the debunking of traditional values and an ever-increasing pressure to be trendy, up-to-date and in fashion. Anomie is thus inherent in almost any highly industrialised society with a liberal democratic regime.

In order to find the prime cause of anomie Parsons reverts to Max Weber's concept of rationalisation: scientific and technological advances are made possible by a critical rationality which inevitably challenges accepted values. The process of rationalisation tends to divide society into those who accept progressive values, and those who are determined to uphold old values and are forced to take a reactionary and even irrational stand against the march of progress. As a conservative Parsons has severe reservations about the rationalising fraction of this dichotomy. He accuses the rationalists of the fallacy of 'misplaced concreteness' which results from the separation of their values and attitudes from the total social system, their patronising attitude towards 'backward' elements within society, and their neglect of vitally important aspects of society such as the family, which does not play a direct role in the productive process. Parsons accuses socialists of being the worst offenders in that they regard an abstract and schematised capitalism as the root of all evil. Capitalism is the original sin of the new religion.

Thus neither liberalism nor socialism are able to provide an orientation in a divided society, and fascism was a violent reaction against these rationalising forces. It condemned capitalism, professed to stand for the old, established values and appealed to the irrational aspects of life which had been ignored by the narrow rationalists. Fascism was thus a kind of reverse image of the process of modernisation.

Parsons's description of anomie in modern society comes close to that of Fromm and, like the Marxist philosopher, Ernst Bloch, he stresses that the rate of modernisation in different sectors is uneven, thus causing further conflicts. Although lacking the refinement of Bloch's 'dialectics of non-simultaneity', this concept of 'imperfect structural integration' does give a certain dynamic to his model. The weakness of this approach, however, is that it places the main stress on the problem of the way in which individuals and groups interpret social change. By concentrating on the ideological aspects, and by failing to develop a dialectical theory of the relationship between ideology and economic and technological change Parsons sees the problem of anomie resulting from the inability of either rationalistic or traditional ideological formations to deal with changed social reality. As Ernst Bloch points out, the inability of ideologies to 'explain' reality is largely due to an underlying social antagonism resulting from the uneven development which Parsons mentions, but does not satisfactorily relate to the problem of ideology and its functionality or dysfunctionality. The historical process is thus reduced to being little more than the gradual debunking of normative social values.

That fascism triumphed in Germany and took on the most violent form must be, for Parsons, the result of the specific problems of German society which makes Germany distinct from the United States or Britain. The characteristic distinguishing marks of German society are militarism, feudalism, authoritarianism, bureaucratisation and a rigid sense of hierarchy. All these factors render German society particularly rigid and thus aggravate the general tendency of modern societies to suffer from anomie. The Germans became terrified of loss of status, and particularly of proletarianisation, because of this firmly reinforced sense of hierarchy. Secondly, industrialisation resulted in the patriarchal father becoming an economic object, and thus his authority was undermined as his relationship to the productive process underwent a fundamental change.

Unlike the more extreme proponents of an autonomic theory of fascism Parsons does not ignore the role of elites and vested interests. He points out that in seriously divided societies these groups are liable to pursue their interests by intrigue and conspiracy, and thus the traditional German elites were quite willing to come to terms with the fascists. The industrialists hoped that the fascists would destroy the threat of the labour movement, and the threatened middle classes were attracted by the fascist emphasis on traditional values and their vague and reactionary anti-capitalism. Junkers and militarists also hoped that they could retain and enhance their influence by associating with the fascists.

The situation in Germany was further exacerbated by exogenous factors: the treaty of Versailles, inflation, depression, and 'economic and political problems'. But these factors merely accelerated and intensified the feelings of anomie, they did not cause them; they are thus not central to Parsons's theory of fascism.

The major theoretical problem for Parsons is to fit the various parts of his theory of fascism together. This he attempts to do with the concept of 'romanticism', a collection of desires and aspirations which cannot be satisfied within existing society. German society, unlike Anglo-Saxon society, was unable to contain and channel these romantic aspirations, because it was too rigid, lacked individualism, and was less practical. The suppression of women and the formality and status consciousness of marriage allowed for no adequate outlet for romantic love. Thus fascism is seen as a romantic revolt against rationalisation. Parsons takes off from the real world of economic, social and political change and, by refusing to analyse the role of classes, groups and interests, he ends up with a vague and ever-more abstract collection of often contradictory ideas. He is thus unable to provide a theory of fascism, although his attempt to do so is both interesting and instructive.

The most far-reaching and developed middle-class theory of fascism is that of Seymour Martin Lipset. In this version of the theory the middle class is particularly susceptible to fascism because it is threatened by big capital from above and the organised labour movement from below. Liberalism, which attempted to overcome these problems by moderate reform and by intervention to maintain a degree of freedom in the economy, had failed. Fascism was thus a middle-class movement designed to guarantee the status and the prosperity of the middle class in a world which was increasingly inimical to its aspirations and position. Fascism is the extremism of the middle.

Lipset accepts that capitalist society is divided into three classes, and that each of these three classes can espouse an ideology that is either moderate or extremist. Liberalism and fascism are the moderate and extremist ideologies of the middle class, social democracy and communism of the industrial working class and the poorer peasantry, conservatism and right-wing radicalism the variants of the big bourgeoisie and landowners. At first sight this tidy model of social and political classifications appears plausible. But it leaves too many questions unanswered. The close identification of the big bourgeoisie and landowners with fascism cannot be explained, and Lipset's argument that Italian fascism was untypical is hardly convincing. The distinction between right-wing radicalism and fascism is also unclear: Austrian fascism is thus characterised as conservative or right-wing extremist fascism, a curious hybrid beast that casts serious doubts on the usefulness of Lipset's model. His attempt to define conservatism is not particularly helpful. Conservatives are said to be conservative, in other words they are not revolutionaries. They wish to preserve or revive cultural or economic institutions, and are prepared to make political changes in order to achieve this aim. As the cultural and economic interests of the bourgeoisie are never analysed, this definition amounts to little more than an empty tautology, and it is certainly not helpful in providing a clue to the relationship between conservative elites and fascist movements.

In attempting to discover the relationship between class position and the form of extremism Lipset distinguishes between the political intolerance of the lower classes, caused by a mixture of ignorance and insecurity, and the economic intolerance of the middle and upper classes caused by the threat from above and below and which is coupled with political tolerance. This argument reveals the ideological *parti pris* of Lipset's concept of tolerance. Tolerance is seen as a specifically bourgeois virtue which can only function at times of relative economic stability and which should not be threatened by the demands of the working class or the monopolists. The existing social order is thus justified by the existence of tolerance as a class-specific virtue. The elite is seen as essentially passive, the masses authoritarian and anti-democratic, problems of social domination and control are abstracted and trivialised, and social crises psychologised. Rather than deliver a satisfactory theory of fascism Lipset is obliged to confess that fascism was the result of unfortunate historical circumstances and the rejection of traditional and liberal structures. It is thus much more of an attempt to justify existing society than it is to explain fascism.

The most powerful support for the middle-class theory of fascism comes not from the ambitious but flawed arguments of Parsons and Lipset, but rather from the empirical analysis of the membership and voters attracted by fascist parties. From a number of detailed studies it is clear that the overwhelming majority of the membership of the N.S.D.A.P. came from middle-class elements who were threatened and uncertain. The same is true of the Italian fascist party. Studies of the Reichstag elections between 1928 and 1933 show that the democratic middle-class parties lost 80 per cent of their voters to the N.S.D.A.P. Only the catholic centre party was able to maintain its share of the vote. The right-wing D.N.V.P., the heirs to the old conservative party, lost relatively few votes to the fascists, and the working-class vote was largely held by the social democrats and the communists, their relative share of that vote often changing dramatically. Lipset is thus perfectly correct to characterise the typical German fascist as a middle-class, independent, male protestant, living on the land or in a small town, who had previously voted for a party of the centre.

It is thus established that the fascist mass parties were largely organisations of the petit bourgeoisie, and further that a mass party was one of the distinguishing marks of fascism which gave it a pseudo-democratic dimension thus setting it apart from other forms of extreme, right-wing regime. It is also clear that fascist regimes did not pursue policies which were helpful to the petit bourgeoisie, and that the social strata which had helped provide the mass base for the regime gained little from fascism once it was in power. This fundamental contradiction between the mass basis and the fascist functional elite is one of the most perplexing and important questions about the nature of fascism. The middle-class theory of fascism refuses to analyse this contradiction, and in effect exculpates the capitalist elites by refusing to question the functionality of fascism. On the other hand the extreme Marxist-Leninist view sees the mass base as largely irrelevant, being little more than the dupes of monopoly capitalism.

The relationship between mass party and elite, between middle class and fascism, must not be seen in terms of the primacy of the one over the other, nor is it a question of cause and effect, but rather in terms of a dialectical interdependence within the framework of monopoly capitalist society. Lipset's liberal society combines political tolerance with a degree of economic intolerance. In other words, those sectors of society that were threatened by the monopolies were integrated into society. The majority provided the political legitimation to a system which objectively was antagonistic to its true interests. It is precisely this ability to overcome social antagonisms and to provide a general support for the domination of society by an elite which gives liberal society its particular strength. The domination of society by monopoly capitalism is most effectively and painlessly secured by a liberal democratic society.

In a situation of economic and social crisis this system of integration begins to collapse, and society is revealed as antagonistic. The veil of false consciousness begins to lift. The middle class begins to demand a middle policy between the extremes of big capital and organised labour, and appeals for 'national unity' directed by a strong national government, which will abolish the mounting class conflict between capital and labour. The failure of the democratic system to provide this national unity is taken as proof that democracy itself is the villain and must be destroyed. The fascist parties promised a third way between monopoly capitalism and socialism, and thus to save the middle class from the ghastly dilemma of siding with the monopolists to destroy the threat from the left, or with the working class in order to destroy capitalism.

Both Italian fascism and the N.S.D.A.P. under the leadership of Hitler were violent counter-revolutionary movements which subscribed to a virulent nationalism, and, in the case of the German fascists, a vicious racism. But both parties contained in their programmes certain anti-monopolistic and 'socialist' elements which had a distinct appeal to certain sectors of society. Such ideas appealed to young university graduates who saw little chance of employment, to low-paid white-collar workers who were threatened by unemployment or by the fear of losing such little status as they had and becoming blue-collar workers, to small businessmen who feared the irresistible competition of big business, and to the small farmer who feared the big landowner. For such people fascism was indeed, as Radek had argued, the socialism of the petit bourgeoisie. The fascist parties articulated a widespread rejection of the modern world, industrialisation, urbanisation, rationalisation, democracy and liberalism, but within this ill-conceived and contradictory ideology there were two main currents. To the right, the fascism of Mussolini and Hitler, the party worked in close alliance with the leaders of industry and finance, worked with the bourgeois parties of the right, and did not seek to destroy the state apparatus, but rather to use it for its own purposes. Such a policy was irreconcilable with 'left-wing' fascism, which in Italy had a strong anarcho-syndicalist content, and in Germany was marked by a reactionary anti-capitalism. The closer the links between the fascists and the traditional elites the stronger became its anti-socialist thrust, and its anti-capitalism became increasingly mild. In Germany the left wing, led by Gregor Strasser, was particularly powerful and posed a serious problem to Hitler's leadership. Hitler's passionate anti-semitism here proved to be a powerful ideological means of integrating the party. 'Capitalism' became equated with 'Jewish capitalism', and anti-capitalist feelings could be directed against a minority group. The anti-modernists were further appeased by fascist paintings of blonde, blue-eyed peasant girls in plaits, by parades of women with distaffs and spinning wheels, by folk-dancing, traditional costumes and the literature of 'blood and soil'.

The fascist left in Germany fought back against this attempt to purge the movement of its petit bourgeois socialism. They could not accept that socialism was nothing more than the invention of the 'Jew Marx', and part of the perfidious attempt by world Jewry to destroy the Aryan race. To them it was the result of the injustices and wickedness of the capitalist system, which in its monopolist phase had also become a threat to the middle classes. The fascist left, however, rejected the socialist solution to the problem of capitalism, insisted on strict class divisions and dreamt of a return to pre-monopolistic conditions, or even to the guilds and estates of the Middle Ages. Their programme was thus utopian, illusory, and absurd. Fascism could therefore offer no realistic alternative to monopoly capitalist society, it could only make political changes and attempt to find new methods of social integration in a society that appeared to be on the verge of disintegration.

With the onset of the Depression it was to a large extent the small businessmen who were attracted by fascism, for the shopkeepers and craftsmen stood to lose everything. These men were not attracted by the fascist left and proved the strongest support for Hitler's leadership. As the party grew rapidly from the summer of 1929 it became an increasingly attractive partner in the eyes of the established elites, which now hoped to use it to destroy the labour movement and neutralise the dissatisfactions and aggressions of the petit bourgeoisie. Money began to pour in from industry, thus directly strengthening Hitler's hold over the party. The *Führerprinzip* was also further reinforced by the sociological make-up of the party. The rootless, threatened, frightened lumpen-bourgeoisie that flocked to the N.S.D.A.P. for protection and salvation wanted to be told what to do, they looked up for guidance, for they had little that was positive to offer themselves. From 1930 Hitler began to crush the left wing of his party, which now threatened both his leadership and his hard-won alliance with his new supporters. The left wing's publishing house, the *Kampfverlag*, was disbanded. Their foreign spokesman, Reventlow, was pushed into the background, as was their economic expert Gottfried Feder, whose ideas on the tyranny of interest had impressed Hitler so much in his early days. When Gregor Strasser attempted to form a coalition with General Schleicher and the unions in December 1932 he was forced to resign.

Hitler's alliance with the old elites of industry, the army and the bureaucracy, blocked the way to a fascist revolution which so many of the rank and file wished. When the euphoria after 30 January 1933 wore off many members were bitter and resentful that so little had changed. The party programme against the monopolies and the chain stores was not implemented. The land reform that had been promised was shelved. The S.A. was resentful of the army, which they had hoped to replace. A popular saying was that the Pg. (*Parteigenosse* – party member) had become a Pj. (*Postenjäger* – place hunter), and indeed the promise of 'jobs for the boys' in a vast fascist bureaucracy was one of the great appeals of fascism, as Gramsci had been one of the first to emphasise. But these jobs were limited, for the regime appreciated the support and the expertise of the established bureaucracy. The fascist party had done its duty. It had achieved power with the minimum of disruption. Its left wing now threatened a 'second revolution' which the Reichswehr was delighted to help crush at the behest of the fascist leadership. With the 'Röhm putsch' of 1934 the N.S.D.A.P. lost its last remaining vestiges of independence, and became the tool of the leadership and little more than a useful means of integration and control. Its membership ceased to be dominated by radical petit bourgeois elements and it became a state party representing a broad cross-section of German society.

The fascist mass movement, with its demands for a return to past forms of economic and social organisation, subscribed to a programme which was a practical impossibility and fraught with contradictions. After all, a modern military force could not be developed so as to fight a modern imperialist war by a nation devoted to folk-dancing and spinning wheels. For a fascist movement to come to power it must accommodate this fanatical and irrational revolt against social reality, it must realise that such a movement can offer no genuine alternative to existing society, and must be channelled by the leadership to accept an alliance with the elite of the society which they theoretically reject, for it is only through such an alliance that the fascists are able to realise their foreign and domestic political ambitions. Had the leadership failed to control and later to eliminate the left wing of the party, fascism would never have come to power, for it would not have been able to win the support of the functional elite which was vital for its success. As Reinhard Kühnl, the historian of the national socialist left, has pointed out, the left wing has a purely demagogic and destructive function. Its programme could never have been realised for it was based on an objective impossibility.

The close relationship between the capitalist elite and the fascists analysed in the previous chapter, coupled with the objective impossibility of left-wing fascism, does not mean that fascism was simply the open terrorist dictatorship of the most reactionary, chauvinist and imperialist elements of finance capital as Dimitroff had argued. Although fascism saw the terroristic implementation of reactionary, chauvinist and imperialist policies within the framework of monopoly capitalism, it was more than the mere implementation of the policies of a group or groups of monopolists. Such a policy had been attempted but had failed between 1930 and 1933. A mass basis was needed for the system to survive, and the old elites were prepared to surrender political power to the fascists in an attempt to save the system. For all the identity of aims the industrialists, bankers, bureaucrats and soldiers often had to accept political directives from the fascist leadership which they resented, which hurt the interests of certain sectors or which were even dysfunctional to the system. In the last resort the Dimitroff definition of fascism makes the existence of a mass party irrelevant to a fascist regime. We have seen, however, that the mass party played a vital role in the rise of fascism, both in making fascism a worthwhile partner to the elites and as a means of integrating and controlling anti-socialist opposition elements within a monopoly capitalist society.

A characteristic of fascism is thus a change from an opposition party articulating however confusingly and unrealistically the fears and aspirations of middle-class elements that feel threatened from above and below, into a party in power which plainly pursues the policies of the big bourgeoisie, which ignores the interests of the rank and file and which even pursues policies diametrically opposed to their vital needs. This change was made possible in part because of the divisions within the ranks of fascistoid middle-class elements and the lack of a clearly articulated class position. Fascism in power could easily exploit these divisions and weaknesses, and the contradiction between the social basis and the social function of fascism could be overcome with relatively little difficulty – expulsions in the case of the Italian party, a swift and limited blood bath in Germany.

Reluctant to join forces with the anti-capitalist working class, the petit bourgeoisie complained about monopolisation but continued to support the social system which had brought it about. Thus its power as an opposition force was strictly limited. The contradiction within fascism was thus based on false consciousness, and could therefore never reach a degree of intensity that might threaten the regime. Fascism in power found it therefore relatively easy to control the masses by such organisations as the *Deutsche Arbeitsfront*, the S.A., the *N.S.-Frauenschaft, Kraft durch Freude, fasci femminili, opera nazionale dopolavoro*, or the *fasci giovinili*. It was the remarkable achievement of the fascist parties that they exploited the tensions and frustrations within society to create organisations that were foreign to the traditions of bourgeois society, and in so doing integrated opposition elements to accept an identity of aims with the established elites which they professed to oppose, and to oblige the elites to accept those forms of domination which they had been unable or unwilling to apply. The mass parties gave the fascist leadership their exceptional power and authority and enabled them to masquerade as the true representatives of the national will. This gave the regimes added strength and enabled the old elites to profit from fascism and pursue their aims. The result was a partnership. The monopolies did not simply pay the piper and call the tune. Indeed the dictators at times behaved like sorcerers' apprentices and showed a degree of independence and wilfulness that mocks the simplistic theory that fascism was merely the direct rule of monopoly capitalism.

# Chapter 7

# Fascism and Bonapartism

The failure of the Third International to provide an adequate theory of fascism, and the resulting inadequacies of communist policies to combat fascism, prompted many Marxist thinkers to reconsider the problem. Among many such attempts the most successful was that of August Thalheimer, one of the leading intellectuals of the German party. Thalheimer based his analysis of fascism on Marx's writing on Louis Napoleon, particularly the '18th Brumaire of Louis Bonaparte' and 'The Civil War in France'.* He was careful not to confuse fascism with Bonapartism, and he did not force contemporary reality into a historical mould. He realised that Marx had an exceptional theoretical understanding of the problem of a counter-revolutionary movement within bourgeois society, and that there were indeed striking similarities between Bonapartism and fascism in the historical relationship between classes, in the political practice, and in the dynamics of the two forms of reactionary regime.

Bonapartism resulted from the fears of the French bourgeoisie that the parliamentary regime was no longer able to guarantee their interests. Working-class revolt in 1848 had made them uncertain and fearful, and they now looked for a drastic solution to their predicament. Parliamentary rule, the great political achievement of the bourgeoisie, now

---

* *Marx Engels Werke*, vol. 8, p. 111; vol. 7, p. 9.

became a danger to the hegemony of the class that had created it. What had been praised as 'liberal' now had to be condemned as 'socialist'. The bourgeoisie had to be saved from the consequences of its own rule. As Marx wrote: 'In order to save its purse, it must forfeit the crown.'* Bonapartism was thus bourgeois in its class character, for it was a regime designed to preserve the economic and social position of the bourgeoisie. But for this to happen the bourgeoisie was prepared to relinquish political power to the independent power of executive authority.

The social basis of support for Bonapartism was the small peasants. The redistribution of land had been one of the great achievements of the French Revolution, but it had now become a serious hindrance to further development in the agricultural sector. Large estates with capital-intensive farming were now required. The peasantry was determined to resist the progress of agricultural capitalism, and looked for firm leadership to save them. Unlike the revolutionary working class the peasants upheld the bourgeois principle of private property, but they needed help against the monopolising tendencies of big capital. Because they lacked any political or economic organisation that might enforce their class interests they did not form a class, strictly speaking. Lacking their own representation they had to be represented. As Marx said: 'The political influence of the small-holding peasants, therefore, finds its expression in the executive power subordinating society to itself.'†

Support for the Bonapartist regime came not only from the small-holding peasants, but also from the political movement – the society of 10 December. Marx described the society in characteristically vivid language:

On the pretext of founding a benevolent society the *Lumpenproletariat* of Paris had been organised into secret sections, each section being led by Bonapartist agents, with a Bonapartist general at the head of the whole. Alongside decayed *roués* with dubious means of subsistence and of dubious origin, alongside ruined and adventurous offshoots of the bourgeoisie, were vagabonds, discharged soldiers, discharged jail-birds, escaped galley slaves, swindlers, mountebanks, *lazzaroni*, pick-pockets, tricksters, gamblers, *maquereaux*, brothelkeepers, porters, *literati*, organ grinders, rag-pickers, knife-grinders, tinkers, beggars – in short, the whole indefinite, disintegrated mass, thrown hither and thither, which the French term *la bohème*.

* Ibid. vol. 8, p. 154.        † Ibid. vol. 8, p. 199.

The composition of this group is not haphazard, for it provides a home for the *déclassés* of all classes who live in a kind of ideological no-man's-land. Yet for all its revolutionary talk this grouping can never be revolutionary, for although it may represent to a certain degree the negation of the bourgeois class principle, yet it remains within this principle. *La bohème* is no more opposed to bourgeois society than a thief is opposed to private property.

Napoleonic ideology was skilfully used to hold together this extraordinarily divided state. The peasantry appreciated Napoleon III's claim to stand apart from the struggles between capital and labour. The support of the working class was courted by referring to parliament as an instrument of bourgeois class rule and by claiming that the destruction of parliament was thus in the interest of the proletariat. Napoleon also claimed to act in the interests of the propertied classes because he upheld their superiority over the working class. Finally the idea of the pursuit of national glory was used to bind all the classes together.

Similarities with fascism are striking. Fascism was not, of course, a peasant movement, but the position of the small-holding peasant in France was similar to that of the urban petit bourgeoisie in Italy and Germany. The social basis of Bonapartism and fascism was a sector of society which had at one time, at the beginning of the process of industrialisation, been revolutionary, but which was now threatened by the further development of industrial society and had therefore become counter-revolutionary. Both the peasantry and the petit bourgeoisie were unable to articulate their common aspirations and frustrations, because both groups comprised isolated individuals who lacked any sense of class solidarity. Thus both groups were willing to submit to the will and bidding of a saviour.

The fascist parties, like Louis Napoleon's society of 10 December, provided a happy home for the *déclassés* of all classes, for the rootless and the bitter. But there was clearly a difference of degree. Fascist regimes were backed by mass parties, Louis Napoleon by a small band. This is due to different historical circumstances and the different degree to which the contradictions which gave rise to the need for a Bonapartist or fascist regime had developed. For Thalheimer the mass party was a mixed blessing to a fascist regime. On the one hand it strengthened its independence, but on the other hand it intensified the problem of the contradiction between the party which represented the aspirations of the masses and the particular interests of the ruling class.

Thalheimer's argument that the fascist party need not always have identical interests with the ruling class distinguishes him from the theorists of the Third International with their heteronomic theory of fascism. Thalheimer's idea was based partly on direct observations of fascist regimes, but also on Marx's view that Bonapartism witnessed the creation of a relatively independent executive state power. This notion has caused a number of problems to Marxist writers, for if state power could become relatively independent it was obviously no longer possible to catagorise the state as the executive committee of the ruling class. It also raised the problem of the relationship between 'basis' and 'superstructure' in Marx's thought, for it suggested that the relationship could, under certain circumstances, be weighted in favour of the superstructure, thus reversing the normal emphasis on the basis. Marx believed that the bourgeois state was characterised not only by the economic domination by the bourgeoisie, but also by the tendency for state power to become independent, and thus he insisted that it was necessary for the revolutionary proletariat not only to destroy the economic power of the bourgeoisie, but also to smash the state machinery. Thus for Marx the independence of the state machine is structurally immanent within capitalist society. It is not the characteristic of a particular historical epoch but rather the result of the intensification of the contradictions between capital and labour. Bonapartism was thus one form of a characteristic mode of rule in bourgeois society, as it would seem that the 'usurpatory dictatorship of the government apparatus' was the only possible way in which the bourgeoisie would be able to continue its domination over the proletariat. But Marx was also insistent that the state was not 'suspended in mid-air'. Bonapartism was a form of bourgeois rule, it is just that the relatively independent executive determined the way in which the economic domination of society by the bourgeoisie should be organised. This process, which Engels described as that whereby the state ceases to serve society and becomes its master, is not of course the equivalent of fascism, but it certainly makes fascism more probable and makes it more difficult to combat fascistic tendencies in the modern state.

Thalheimer stressed a further similarity between Bonapartism and fascism – the foreign policy of the two regimes. Louis Napoleon attempted to paper over the contradictions within his regime with his foreign adventures. For Marx and Engels Napoleon's escapades in Syria and Mexico, in the Crimea and China, against Austria and Germany were a necessary consequence of his form of rule. A regime which claimed to stand above the divisions of class needed to find some way of concealing these divisions. Dramatic acts of foreign policy were deliberately designed to unite the country and take people's minds off the pressing problems of the day. Thus Bonapartist foreign policy can be seen as a safety valve which reduces domestic political tensions.

Marx stressed that Bonapartism had been preceded by an attempt by the working class to take bourgeois society by storm which had failed and had succeeded in filling the bourgeoisie with fear. Bourgeois ideological formations were suffering from a profound crisis, and there were severe divisions within the hegemonic bloc. Thalheimer wrote: 'A severe defeat of the proletariat in an acute social crisis is one of the preconditions of Bonapartism.'* If this analysis were to be applied to fascism then it was clear that fascism followed the defeat of the working class, and if that were true then the Third International was quite wrong in thinking of fascism as a defensive move by the bourgeoisie and the strategy of 'social fascism' was therefore seriously misguided.

A further difference between Thalheimer's definition of fascism and that of the Third International, differences which were to lead to his expulsion from the K.P.D. and the International in 1929, was his reading of Marx's contention that Bonapartism is the 'ultimate' form of bourgeois class domination. For the International fascism was the end of the road for capitalism, it was the last hideous death agony of a moribund system which would be replaced by socialism. Thalheimer pointed out that if one takes 'ultimate' to mean 'final' then Marx was clearly talking rubbish. How was it possible that bourgeois power had survived almost untrammelled in the Third Republic? Nor was Bonapartism 'ultimate' in the sense of being the most highly developed form of bourgeois domination, for French capitalism was not particularly far advanced and was still in a state of free competition. For Marx 'ultimate' was used in terms of the totality of class relationships. Thalheimer argued that Bonapartism was the ultimate form of bourgeois class domination when the bourgeoisie had been faced with the real threat of a proletarian revolution and had exhausted itself in its struggle for the defence of its privileged position. It is a defensive form of bourgeois state power in the face of proletarian revolt, and fascism is a closely similar form of the dictatorship of capital.

Thalheimer's characterisation of fascism as a defensive strategy is open

* *Geg⸱ ⸱ ⸱ len Strom*, no. 32 (1930).

to question and contradicts his contention that it follows the defeat of the working class. He tends to exaggerate the degree to which the state apparatus pursued policies that were contrary to the wishes and needs of the capitalist elites. On both these points his theory needs refining. But the main thrust of his argument was correct. He warned that fascism strengthened the economic and political power of the bourgeoisie, so that the collapse of fascism was likely to be followed by the restoration of bourgeois parliamentary democracy, and that socialists should be prepared for that eventuality rather than dream that socialism was the inevitable outcome of the collapse of fascism. He attacked the view that fascism was the 'open dictatorship of the bourgeoisie' because fascism was but one of the forms which that open dictatorship could take. Nor could the weakening of the authority of parliament and a strengthening of the executive branch of government, which is characteristic of most liberal democratic countries, be taken as equivalent to fascism. Nor should the presidential regime of Brüning be confused with fascism, for a qualitative and quantitative leap was needed before it could be considered fascist. By destroying parliamentary democracy Brüning paved the way for fascism, but he was not himself a fascist.

Thalheimer never equated fascism and Bonapartism, for they were different and distinct counter-revolutionary regimes. He did, however, use Marx's discussion of Bonapartism as the starting point of his own investigation of fascism. It was General Schleicher who attempted to establish a Bonapartist regime in Germany by trying to create a military and police dictatorship that would co-operate with the organised working class and other disgruntled sectors. Such a regime cannot work in a highly developed industrial society, for the divisions and tensions are too great to be overcome in a crisis situation. In a country like Argentina under Peron such a form was possible; in a more developed state the working class has to be crushed. This was precisely the major difference between Bonapartism and fascism. Fascism was a totalitarian, one-party system, which smashed the labour movement because Bonapartist methods could not control such a seriously divided society.

Another leading Marxist thinker who based his theory of fascism to a considerable extent on Marx's theory of Bonapartism was Trotsky. It is a constant theme in Trotsky's writings that the petit bourgeoisie is incapable of independent political action, and that it was this class which formed the mass base of fascism. Communist parties would therefore have to win over this class to the socialist camp, otherwise they would join the ranks of the fascists. The Comintern's theory of social fascism was simply driving the petit bourgeoisie into the arms of the fascists, and made any effective anti-fascist policy impossible.

Contrary to the Third International, Trotsky distinguished between the regimes of Brüning, Papen and Schleicher and the fascists. To Schleicher's regime he attached the appropriate label 'Bonapartist'. The regime enjoyed a degree of independence from society which had not been achieved by Brüning, who had operated with an uneasy parliamentary majority which enjoyed the tacit support of the Nazis as well as the social democrats. It was an officially 'apolitical' regime based on a military and police dictatorship. It attempted to win some support from the working class, and was an essentially inactive regime designed to maintain the status quo. Trotsky thus argued that German Bonapartism was a barrier against fascism, for the regime acted as a kind of umpire and policeman between the left and the right, trying to stop either side from becoming too powerful and hindering an open civil war.

Bonapartism, in Trotsky's view, was characterised by its lack of mass support, although we have seen that Marx insisted that it enjoyed the backing of the small-holding peasants and Schleicher had made a desperate bid for mass support. Fascism differs from Bonapartism in this version, in that it has a mass following. Trotsky, however, pointed out that because of the alliance between the monopoly capitalist elite and the fascist leadership a fascist regime could not continue to be based on social demagogy and petit bourgeois terror. Fascist regimes are thus obliged to control, restrain and even silence the masses who supported them on the way to power. Fascism thus loses its mass support, and becomes bureaucratised. When this happens it is no longer fascism but a form of Bonapartism — 'Bonapartism of fascist origin'. Thus Trotsky's theory of Bonapartism led him to make the serious error that fascism was a temporary phenomenon. Once fascism had crushed its radical wing and become Bonapartist it was, for Trotsky, well on the way to decline.

Thus in Trotsky's view fascism is an attempt by the leaders of finance capital to find an alternative form of domination to bourgeois democracy, which had failed to guarantee their ascendancy. The petit bourgeoisie is mobilised and radicalised so that bourgeois democracy might be overthrown, but once this happens the petit bourgeois mass movement becomes a potential threat. In the period of bourgeois ascendancy the jacobins had been used by the bourgeoisie as the 'plebeian solution' to their struggle against feudal society, now in the period of bourgeois decline fascism was a new form of this 'plebian solution'. Fascism was the 'battle organisation of the bourgeoisie during, and in the event of, a civil war. . . . It plays the same role for the bourgeoisie as the organisation of armed insurrection for the proletariat'.* This idea further strengthened Trotsky's belief that fascism was essentially temporary, for just as armed insurrection cannot continue indefinitely, so fascism is bound to return to some form of modified bourgeois legality.

Revolutionary proletarian internationalism was the only answer, in Trotsky's view, to the menace of fascism. Trotsky argued that the social patriotism of the Stalinist theory of 'socialism in one country' made effective international proletarian action impossible, and blinded the Comintern to the revolutionary possibilities that abounded. His theory of fascism was thus a part of his extraordinary revolutionary optimism which led him to see 'revolutionary situations' even in the most improbable places. Since he believed that fascism was a bourgeois response to a proletarian threat to bourgeois society it was symptomatic of a 'revolutionary situation'. Thus he denounced the Soviet idea of collective security on the grounds that an alliance between the Soviet Union and the bourgeois states against fascism would only encourage the social patriotic tendencies in the German working class. Similarly the proletariat should not support the anti-fascist wing of the national bourgeoisie for this would also strengthen the class collaborationists within the socialist movement. Trotsky therefore denounced the people's fronts of the Spanish type because they dampened the class struggle and, given Trotsky's initial premise on fascism, weakened the anti-fascist forces.

This belief that there was a simple choice between socialist revolution, which would lead to the united socialist states of Europe, or fascism, made Trotsky adopt a variation of the theory of social fascism which he so bitterly castigated in its Soviet form. He denounced the policy of the popular front and collective security for objectively helping the fascists by directly weakening the proletarian forces which alone would be able to combat fascism. He attacked Thaelmann for talking about 'people's revolutions' which he considered to be a fascist concept, typical of the Comintern's refusal to see that the revolution would have to be proletarian or it would be nothing. Nevertheless, he still insisted that there was a profound difference between Stalin's Russia and fascist regimes, although he was never quite certain about the precise nature of the Soviet Union.

* Leo Trotzki, *Gesammelte Werke* (Frankfurt, 1971) p. 721.

Trotsky's theory of fascism suffers from the serious weakness that he was unable or unwilling to analyse in depth the precise nature of the crisis within capitalist society to which fascism was a response. At times he suggested it was due to acute problems of reproduction and capital accumulation in monopoly capitalism, but this did nothing to explain why fascism triumphed in Italy rather than in the more advanced capitalist states. At other times he thought that fascism was due to a purely political crisis, the failure of the bourgeois political process to provide the necessary stability without which the economic system would fail to function at maximum efficiency. At times he even felt that fascism was a sinister invention of the bourgeoisie, in much the same way that Voltaire imagined that the church was the invention of cynical and self-seeking priests. But even more serious was his failure to analyse the role of the petit bourgeoisie in capitalist society. Whereas Marx had argued that the petit bourgeoisie was essentially reactionary, even though it sometimes affected a certain pseudo-revolutionary jargon, and Lenin had always insisted that the petit bourgeoisie could never go beyond an anarchic 'leftism', Trotsky made a major departure from classical Marxism by insisting that the petit bourgeoisie could be won over to the ranks of the revolutionary proletariat if only the communist parties would provide the necessary leadership. Without an adequate understanding of the role and nature of the petit bourgeoisie in advanced capitalism, Trotsky could not comprehend the trajectory of the mass support afforded to fascist movements, and by arguing that the petit bourgeoisie could be revolutionised he was to take totally unrealistic and irresponsible ultra-left positions which vitiated any effective anti-fascist strategy. To condemn all those who supported the popular front, including Stalin, as the 'petit bourgeois agents of capitalism' was as absurd as similar accusations made by the Comintern during the heyday of the theory of social fascism against anti-fascist social democrats.

Trotsky's attempt to use the Marxist theory of Bonapartism to illuminate the problems of fascism is thus less satisfactory than that of Thalheimer. The main reason for this is that Trotsky failed to come to grips with the original theory. Marx saw the characteristics of Bonapartism as the relative independence of the executive authority from the bourgeoisie, the destruction of parliament, the reduction of the bourgeoisie to political nullity, and the creation of a situation whereby the 'sword that is to protect the bourgeoisie hangs over its head like the sword of

Damocles'.* Thalheimer, basing his theory of fascism on this analysis, concluded that fascism was the 'rendering independent of executive power, the political control of the masses, including the bourgeoisie itself, under fascist state power with the social domination of the bourgeoisie and the big landowners'.† Marx, as we have seen, was concerned to emphasise that the bourgeoisie had relinquished direct political power in order to preserve its economic power, and that economic power in turn should not be seen merely in terms of financial power but also as social power – hence the very delicate distinction between economics and politics in Marx's thought. Whereas Marx went to great lengths to examine the social composition of the mass support for Bonapartism, Trotsky insisted that Bonapartism was characterised by a lack of mass support. It is clear that the Marxist definition of Bonapartism could not be applied to the regimes of Brüning or Papen, for the bourgeoisie had certainly not relinquished political power, nor had parliament been given its quietus even though parliamentary democracy had failed to master the crisis and had voluntarily suspended its functions. This confusion led Trotsky to talk of 'pre-Bonapartism', 'pseudo-Bonapartism', 'preventive Bonapartism', 'fascist Bonapartism', and 'senile Bonapartism', thus rendering the concept of Bonapartism so vague as to be of little value as an analytical tool. There is much truth in Trotsky's statement that 'fascism leads to a military and bureaucratic dictatorship of a Bonapartist type', but only if we use Marx's definition of Bonapartism, not Trotsky's.

Thalheimer's skilful use of Marx's theory of Bonapartism as the starting point of his theory of fascism was a major methodological advance which has served as the basis of many valuable later works. It rejects the schematic and undialectical relationship between basis and superstructure which is characteristic of the heteronomic theory of the Third International. But at the same time it does not accept the autonomic approach which sees fascism as being to a large extent independent from economic determinants. This theory, which evolves from a critique of both the heteronomic and the autonomic theories of fascism, is an undogmatic and critical application of the principles of historical materialism which sees the social process as historical, dialectical and rooted in the material world.

In such a theory fascism is seen as a historical phenomenon. As such the

* *Marx Engels Werke*, vol. 8, p. 154.
† In *Gegen den Strom*, no. 32 (1950).

label of fascist cannot be attached to regimes of the distant past, or to extremist right-wing dictatorships in countries which have not experienced the same level of historical development. Thus the theory strictly limits the applicability of the term and increases its heuristic value, unlike those transpolitical theories which see fascism as deeply rooted in human nature and not limited to a specific historical situation. But at the same time it goes beyond the theories of men like Nolte, who see fascism as a phenomenon unique to a specific epoch, and insists that fascism is structurally immanent within advanced capitalism.

Heteronomic theories of fascism run the risk of becoming crudely schematic, from an extreme with the theory that fascism was an inevitable stage through which monopoly capitalism is bound to pass, to the less dogmatic view that fascism is a permanent danger in any capitalist society. In such versions the historical circumstances which led to the rise of fascism in Italy and Germany, but not in England and the United States, are of greatly inferior significance. A syncretic historical materialist theory, such as Thalheimer's, accepts that fascism is an immanent danger within advanced capitalist states, but only becomes a threat and a danger in certain specific historical circumstances. Such an approach is anathema to vulgar-Marxists who wish to reduce the historical process to a straightforward economic determinism. But, as Engels pointed out, such a view was a negation of the dialectical theory which is at the very heart of historical materialism, and rather than examining the reciprocal interaction between various social factors it reduces everything to a simplistic cause and effect. Such a rigidly deterministic theory was also useless as a political weapon, because it implied that the anti-fascist forces were doomed from the outset and that there was nothing that could be done except to prepare for the worst. In the historical materialism of Marx and Engels ample room is left for the individual to make history, even though the circumstances in which he does so may not be of his own choice.

This syncretic theory combines elements of the heteronomic and the autonomic theories, neither of which are satisfactory on their own. Thus Hitler, for example, cannot be regarded either as the fabrication of monopoly capitalists or as a man without any ties who bewitched Germany. He was neither pure accident nor pure design. Conditions were such that Germany needed a dictator. That it happened to be Hitler was largely due to chance. But the question cannot be left there. Hitler offered a political programme which seemed to offer more than the programmes

of any of his rivals – the Brünings, Papens, Schleichers and Strassers, all
of whom tried to fit the role which the historical circumstances demanded. The task of historical materialism is to examine dispassionately
and scientifically the changing economic circumstances, and the way in
which they were reflected in the different programmes, ideologies and
political practice of the time. Only a syncretic theory can examine the
relationship between the heteronomic and the autonomic, the determined and the chance, basis and superstructure, and thus arrive at a theory
which can stand the test of empirical verification, and which alone is
flexible enough to be able to account for the contradictions and the mul-
tiplicity of factors within fascism. The complexity of the structure of
power in fascist states is such that a one-sided theory is bound to be inadequate.

# Chapter 8

# Conclusion: What is Fascism?

Having examined and criticised a number of theories of fascism the time has come to salvage something from the wreckage and to list certain criteria which will enable us to determine whether or not a regime or a political movement can be called fascist.

Firstly, fascism is a phenomenon of developed industrial states. If capitalism has not reached a certain level of development the particular relationships between classes which are characteristic of fascist movements are not possible. Only in advanced capitalism can there be a powerful capitalist class, a large and organised working class with a potentially revolutionary ideology which calls for a radical restructuring of society, and a large petit bourgeoisie which is caught in the contradictions between capital and labour and is unable to find any way out of its social, economic and political dilemmas. Fascism is the product of capitalist society, and for all its anti-capitalist rhetoric, particularly in its early stages, it is unwilling and unable to surpass that society. Fascism is not identical with capitalism, as it is held to be in certain extreme theories of fascism, but there exists between capitalism and fascism a non-identical identity. Fascism is potential within late capitalism, but for that potentiality to become manifest a particular set of historical and social circumstances, which are detailed below, are necessary. Fascism is thus not an inevitable stage through which capitalism is bound to pass.

Secondly, fascist movements are triggered off by a severe socio-economic crisis which threatens a considerable section of society with loss of status and even economic ruin, and which plunges society into a widespread feeling of uncertainty and fear. Confidence in the existing political system and its representatives is shattered and bourgeois-democratic forms no longer seem adequate to master a crisis which appears to threaten the entire structure of society. In every case there is a direct correlation between economic crisis and the rise of fascism, but once again it must be emphasised that fascism is not the automatic response by a capitalist society to an acute crisis. All capitalist countries produced fascist movements after the crash in 1929, but in most of these countries they were movements of the lunatic fringe, and parliamentary regimes, usually of the moderate right, were able to contain and control the crisis without any major quantitative or qualitative changes. It is in countries where the social and political balance is extremely unsteady as a result of specific historical and economic circumstances that a socio-economic crisis of this magnitude can lead to the establishment of a fascist regime.

Thirdly, fascism is a response to a large and organised working class which, through its political parties, whether communist or social democratic, have made significant demands on industry and on the bourgeoisie. Fear of the demands of the working class is a major factor in the mass support for fascist movements and their financing by the capitalist elite. Many felt that it was better to be black (or brown) than red, and the elite was determined to destroy the organisations of the working class. However, fascism is only possible when the socialist working class has suffered severe defeats, such as those in Italy in 1920 and in Germany between 1918 and 1923, and when the socialist parties are so badly divided between themselves as was the case with the communists and the social democrats. Although most fascists saw themselves as defending society against this threat from the left, in fact fascism was, strictly speaking, an offensive against the working class. Fascism attacked a working class that had already been defeated and demoralised. Thus, although a large, organised and menacing working class is a necessary precondition of fascism, it must have spent its forces before fascism can succeed. A united and determined working class is the major safeguard against fascism.

Fourthly, fascism recruits its mass following from a politicised, threatened, and frightened petit bourgeoisie. Artisans, small independent businessmen and farmers who are threatened by monopolisation and severely hurt by the economic crisis flock to the fascists, attracted by their political rhetoric, in the hope of finding economic and social salvation, where they join forces with white-collar workers and lower civil servants who are determined to ward off the immanent threat of being cast down into the ranks of the proletariat. In some instances they are joined by members of the 'aristocracy of labour' who no longer identify with the working class and see in fascism a means of enhancing their social status.

Fifthly, fascist regimes are characterised by an alliance between the fascist party leadership and the traditional elites of industry, banking, the bureaucracy and the military. We have seen that this relationship is a two-way affair. The fascist parties were not simply manipulated by the capitalist elite, and the fascist leadership did not establish the undiluted primacy of politics which reduced the old elites to the level of being the mindless executive organs of political extremists. The community of interests between the functional elite and the fascist leadership resulted in a significant change in the relationship between the leadership and the party. Party members who stressed the social revolutionary aspects of fascism, and who represented the political aspirations of the radical petit bourgeoisie in their demand for a 'second revolution', were purged, and the fascist party stripped of its influence and reduced to the role of social integrator. However, the very existence of a mass party was a powerful weapon which could be used by the leadership, if necessary, to threaten and cajole the old elites when differences over means led to conflict at the top. Attempts by Brüning and Papen to establish authoritarian regimes which had no mass base had failed, so that the fascist solution seemed to be the only viable alternative. The fascist executive enjoyed a certain degree of independence, and often acted in ways that were inimical to sections of industry. The alliance between these two centres of power was thus always close, but it was by no means always harmonious.

Sixthly, the social function of fascism was to stabilise, strengthen and, to a certain degree, transform capitalist property relationships and to ensure the social and economic domination of the capitalist class, which felt threatened, which was divided among itself as to the best means of overcoming the crisis and which was prepared to relinquish some of its political power in order to maintain its privileged position. It can be argued that in this respect fascism is little different from conservatism, which also aims to strengthen and perpetuate the social status quo. The social basis of the support for conservative and extreme right-wing parties is similar. Both factions of the political right subscribe to a vague anti-modernist ideology and a pronounced anti-socialism. Neither show any genuine concern for the fate of their petit bourgeois followers. The significant difference between the two is that conservative regimes, however far to the right they may be, operate within the bounds of legality and of established political practice. Fascist regimes, on the other hand, employ the utmost terror against their opponents in order to achieve their social, political and economic goals. This terror is particularly directed against the organisations of the labour movement. In this limited sense Dimitroff's definition of fascism as open terror by the most reactionary sectors of capitalist society is perfectly correct.

Seventhly, therefore, fascism is a terror regime which dispenses with all the trappings of parliamentary democracy. No opposition whatsoever is allowed, either within or without the fascist movement. The presence of opposition forces, however ineffectual and powerless they may be, is incommensurate with fascism and is evidence of an authoritarian regime which may, nevertheless, contain strong fascist elements. It is, however, inadmissible to take this terror regime as the sole most significant aspect of fascism, as does the theory of totalitarianism. The function and the social basis of this terror distinguish fascism sharply from other forms of terror regime, such as the Soviet Union in the Stalin era.

Eighthly, fascist movements use ideology deliberately to manipulate and divert the frustrations and anxieties of the mass following away from their objective source. Fascist ideology is thus characterised by an emphasis on essentially irrational concepts such as authority, obedience, honour, duty, the fatherland or race. Fascists proclaim the existence of a true community, based on blind obedience and the leadership principle. The main thrust of this ideology is against socialism. It claims to stand for those with property, however small and insignificant that property might be, against those who threaten to take that property away from them. Such a form of anti-socialism amounts to an attack on the very concept of an emancipatory society. The masses are further controlled by the emphasis on the hidden enemies who have sinister designs on society and who threaten the longed-for sense of community. Almost any group, or collection of groups, will fulfil this function, be they Jews or blacks, intellectuals or Jehovah's Witnesses, Gypsies or foreigners. Such groups are relatively weak and unable to defend themselves, and provide excellent scapegoats for the ills and failures of society. Fascists are also able to justify their own shortcomings and failures, and the hardships which they impose on the masses, by conjuring up the vision of a host of enemies at home and abroad who are determined to crush the regime. Thus further sacrifices and efforts can be demanded so that the fascist 'new order' can be finally established.

Ninthly, fascist regimes pursue aggressive and expansionist foreign political aims. This imperialism is justified in terms of military necessity – so that the state may be secure against the menace of its envious neighbours and be prepared for the 'battle of the world-views'. It is also justified in terms of economic necessity – so that economic autarchy can be achieved and the problems of capitalist reproduction overcome. There is also a strong social imperialist moment. The conquest of new land diverts the tensions and frustrations of society away from their objective source, it provides a national purpose and goal, and it can be used to compensate the masses for the privations and the sufferings of the past.

Tenthly, the degree of intensity of any of these above points is determined by the level of capitalist development and the resulting problems which the fascist regime is called upon to overcome. Thus German fascism was far more brutal, aggressive and totalitarian than Italian fascism, because Germany was both a more developed and a more antagonistic society. The crisis of 1933 was thus more acute than the crisis of 1922, and the German fascist regime had at its disposal more sophisticated techniques for mass control, terror and expansion.

If we accept these ten distinguishing marks of fascism how can they be applied to catagorise fascistic regimes? If fascism is a phenomenon of highly developed industrial states, then clearly the military dictatorships of South America and of the under-developed countries of Africa and Asia cannot be termed 'fascist'. Such regimes lack the mass support which characterises fascist movements, even though they are often adept at mobilising the masses. To a considerable extent they uphold a feudal rather than a capitalist mode of production. They do not have the pronounced imperialist ambitions of fascist states, for they are often themselves in a state of imperialist dependency. They frequently lack the instruments of sustained terror and control, and tend rather to indulge in outbursts of uncontrolled brutality and violence. Even the Argentina of Peron, which is frequently described as fascist, was supported by a fundamentally different class alignment and had a quite different function

from a fascist regime. Similarly the bestial counter-revolutionary regime
in Chile, although showing striking similarities with fascism in a number
of aspects, is quite distinct from the fascist model.
The regimes of Spain and Salazar's Portugal and the 'clerical fascism'
of Austria before the *Anschluss* are even closer to the fascist model. But
even here there are significant differences. In Spain the fascist party, the
Falange, never attained the size nor enjoyed the independence of the fascist mass parties in Italy and Germany, and was always controlled and
manipulated by a military clique. Franco's regime initially rested on the
support of the army, the police and the bureaucracy, rather than on the
party. Ideology was the province of the church rather than the Falange.
The socially dominant class was the semi-feudal landowning aristocracy.
The level of capitalist development was modest. In Portugal these restorative and conservative tendencies in the dictatorship were even more
pronounced. The '*Heimwehr* fascism' of Austria, which has yet to be
given a detailed scientific analysis, was also something of a hybrid between fascism and ultra-conservatism. Not until 1938 and the *Anschluss*
did Austrian fascism approach the true fascist model, but that was not the
result of the inner dynamics of Austrian society, but rather the military,
political and economic dominance of Nazi Germany.
    Similarly the right-wing dictatorships of inter-war Europe lacked
many of the essential ingredients of fascist regimes. Poland, Romania,
Greece and Yugoslavia were ruled by varying forms of military dictatorship of a conservative type which, although they suppressed the left,
never went as far as the totalitarian dictatorships of the fascist type. All of
these countries had fascist movements, but they remained on the fringe of
the radical right until, in some cases such as Hungary, Croatia and Slova-
kia, they gained power thanks to German armies of occupation. They
were thus imported regimes which did not reflect the social structure and
political dynamics of the countries which they dominated.
    Although the regimes of Nazi Germany and fascist Italy provide the
best examples of fascism in action it would be a serious mistake to limit a
definition of fascism to these two forms, or even to the period between
the two World Wars. Such a definition would make it impossible to
analyse fascist dangers in the present day. The fact that changing circumstances are liable to produce differences in fascist movements, at least at
the phenomenological level, has led many writers to talk of 'neo-
fascism'.
    It can be argued that the changed circumstances of the capitalist world

since 1945 are such that talk of the end of the epoch of fascism may seem a trifle premature. The capitalist world had been reduced and weakened. The vast increase in the power and influence of the Soviet Union and its dependent states, of China and the whole socialist world which now comprises one third of the world's population has greatly reduced the relative strength of the capitalist world. This tendency is further intensified by the fact that the vast majority of the former colonies have found relative independence. An intolerable strain is placed on the advanced industrial states by the determination of some countries producing essential commodities such as petroleum to command the maximum possible price. In such changing circumstances the classical bourgeois liberal state has undergone some significant changes, and has been obliged to adapt itself to new contingencies. The problem therefore is whether the ruling elites in the advanced capitalist countries have the situation so well in hand and have developed new techniques of government which will make a fascist regime unnecessary, even in situations of grave crisis, or whether an exceptional regime will be established, the techniques of 'crisis management' having failed.

Modern capitalist states are indeed far better equipped than ever before to deal with economic and social crises. The state is prepared to intervene in the workings of the economy to a degree which would have been inconceivable in the inter-war years. The techniques employed to control the effects of economic problems, although in many ways deficient, have greatly improved, and governments are now more ready to use them. The techniques of mass communication have made even more startling advances, enabling a higher degree of control so that an ideological consensus is more easily achieved. Advertising is only one of the more obvious ways in which the individual is manipulated, rendered uncritical and made to absorb a view of the world which serves to maintain and strengthen the status quo.

The similarity between these techniques and those of fascist regimes has led certain ultra-left writers to argue that contemporary capitalist practice is a sinister and concealed form of fascism. Fascism is then seen as that form of domination which maintains the capitalist mode of production in an advanced capitalist society which is threatened by a crisis which challenges and brings into question the principles on which that society is based. In contemporary capitalism, according to this version, opposition groups are fully integrated into the system, the working class is so totally absorbed with economistic concerns that it no longer has any fundamental political demands to make and has completely lost its revolutionary *élan*; parliamentary democracy, freedom of speech and the diverse offerings of the media merely complete the process of control and manipulation. If such an analysis were true then it is of little interest whether contemporary capitalism is labelled 'fascist' or whether one asserts that fascism is an antiquated and outmoded form of control that is no longer necessary. The political consequences that can be drawn from such an analysis are either total resignation as a pseudo-political stance, Eastern mysticism or the rigmarole of the drug culture providing a suitable ideological cover, or irrational outbursts of anarchic putschism. The inevitable failure of either tactic is then used as further evidence of the sinister repressive quality of society, and thus reaffirms the original ideological stance.

Such a reading of the contemporary scene, which commanded a considerable following in the 1960s, has since been proved empirically false. Economic crises, runaway inflation, mass unemployment, racial tensions, the growth of political radicalism and unsuccessful foreign adventures have placed a tremendous strain on many countries. A tendency to strengthen executive power is most noticeable in the Gaullist constitution and in the American presidency, particularly as it was under Nixon. Neither regime could be considered fascist, although they were often accused of it, and their fascistoid tendencies were controlled and contained in large part by the existence of strong pockets of democratic tradition of both a liberal and a socialist nature, which put up a determined resistance to any further encroachments on those liberties and freedoms without which no anti-fascist struggle is possible.

A new fascism is bound to adapt itself to a new situation. This is already apparent in the fascistic movements such as the N.P.D. in Germany, the M.S.I. in Italy or the National Front in Britain. Their style is not as rowdy and violent as that of their predecessors. They are more concerned to appear respectable. Anti-semitism, although often present, is less pronounced. Immigrant workers are frequently blamed for economic problems such as unemployment. Anti-communism takes the place of anti-capitalism. Fascist mass-movements, if they reappear, will probably be more restrained and civilised, but they will be no less menacing. When the manipulation of mass opinion is no longer sufficient to maintain the consensus then the state repression of the opposition groups may well be deemed necessary. Again this need not imply the physical brutality of previous fascist regimes, but may well be of a more subtle and insidious nature. For all the talk of 'structurally immanent state fascism' a mass party, a charismatic leader and a distinct ideology will still be necessary. The nature of all three components is likely to be quite distinct from their historical forms. Such differences combined with a changed economic, political, social and psychological situation may, perhaps, make it more meaningful to speak of 'neo-fascism'. A theory of neo-fascism would take the essential features of the fascism of the past, examine how these factors are likely to have changed, and see under what socio-economic crisis situations in contemporary advanced capitalism such drastic measures are likely to be employed. But such a task lies outside the scope of this present work.

Thus the danger of fascism is still with us. Contrary to the commonly held belief, the dictatorships of the underdeveloped world, although they have clearly learnt much from fascist practice, are not themselves fascist. The regimes of Generals Pinochet and Amin, for example, differ in many essential points from our model of fascism. This does not make them in any sense less revolting and inhuman, but to analyse such regimes in terms of fascism does nothing to provide a true understanding of the nature and dynamics of such systems of domination. It is rather in the highly developed capitalist states that the fascist potential continues to exist. The socio-economic system which produced fascism to overcome its difficulties still exists, the problems which it faces still remain acute. A society which restricts its democratic practice to the functioning of the parliamentary system, and which denies the extension of such democratic forms to vital sections of society including the economic sector is ever prone, under certain specific conditions, to resort to fascism. The struggle against fascism can thus only be effective if it is also a struggle for the extension and the deepening of democratic forces. Such an inhuman, repressive and tyrannical system can only be combated by the determination to strengthen and extend the humane, emancipatory and democratic forces within society. Anti-fascism is thus part of the struggle for the emancipatory society, and an analysis of fascism an essential precondition for effective action.

# Bibliography

K. ADLER and T. G. PATERSON, 'Red Fascism – The Merger of Nazi Germany and Soviet Russia in the American Image of Totalitarianism', *American Historical Review* (April 1970).

W. ALFF, *Der Begriff Faschismus* (Frankfurt, 1971).

G. ANSALDO, 'La piccola borghesia', *Il Lavoro* (3 June 1923).

HANNAH ARENDT, *The Origins of Totalitarianism* (New York, 1951).

M. ASCOLI and A. FEILER, *Fascism for Whom?* (New York, 1938).

G. BATAILLE, 'La Structure psychologique du fascisme', *La Critique sociale* (June 1933, March 1934).

OTTO BAUER, HERBERT MARCUSE and ARTHUR ROSENBERG, *Faschismus und Kapitalismus. Theorien über die sozialen Ursprünge und die Funktion des Faschismus* (Frankfurt, 1967).

CHARLES BETTELHEIM, *L'Economie allemande sous le nazisme* (Paris, 1946).

BERNHARD BLANKE, REIMUT REICHE and JÜRGEN WERTHE, 'Die Faschismustheorie der D.D.R.', *Das Argument*, 33 (1965).

ERNST BLOCH, *Vom Hazard zur Katastrophe, politische Aufsätze aus den Jahren 1934–1939* (Frankfurt, 1972).

——, *Erbschaft dieser Zeit* (Frankfurt, 1973).

I. BONOMI, *Dal socialismo al fascismo* (Rome, 1924).

F. BORKENAU, 'Zur Soziologie des Faschismus', *Archiv für Sozialwissenschaften und Sozialpolitik* (February 1933).

P. H. BOX, *Three Master Builders and Another: Studies in Modern Revolutionary and Liberal Statesmanship* (Philadelphia, 1925).

KARL-DIETRICH BRACHER, *Die Auflösung der Weimarer Republik* (Villingen, 1964).

——, *Die deutsche Diktatur* (Cologne, 1969).

RICHARD M. BRICKNER, *Is Germany Incurable?* (Philadelphia, 1943).

MARTIN BROSZAT, *Der Staat Hitlers* (Munich, 1969).

HANS BUCHHEIM, *Totalitarian Rule* (Middletown, 1968).

R. BUROWES, 'Totalitarianism: The Revised Standard Version', *World Politics* (1969).

J. M. CAMMET, 'Communist Theories of Fascism, 1920–1935', *Science and Society*, 2 (1967).

R. DEL CARRIA, *Proletari senza rivoluzione. Storia delle classi subalterne italiane dal 1860 al 1950* (Milan, 1966).

F. L. CARSTEN, *The Rise of Fascism* (London, 1967).

C. CASUCCI (ed.), *Il fascismo. Antologia di scritti critici* (Bologna, 1961).

RICHARD CHRISTIE and MARIE JAHODA, *Studies in the Scope and Method of 'The Authoritarian Personality'* (New York, 1954).

MANFRED CLEMENZ, *Gesellschaftliche Ursprunge des Faschismus* (Frankfurt, 1972).

——, 'Staatsfaschistische Tendenzen im Spätkapitalismus', *Kursbuch*, 31 (May 1973).

S. B. CLOUGH, *Economic History of Modern Italy* (London, 1964).

EBERHARD CZICHON, *Wer verhalf Hitler zur Macht?* (Cologne, 1967).

——, 'Das Primat der Industrie im Kartell der N.S.-Macht', *Das Argument*, 47 (1968).

RALF DAHRENDORF, *Society and Democracy in Germany* (New York, 1967).

P. DAVILA, 'Charakteristik des italiensichen Faschismus und das balkanische Faschismus', *La Fédération Balkanique* (1 April 1929).

JANE DEGRAS (ed.), *The Communist International, 1919–1943*, 3 vols (London, 1956–65).

M. H. DOBB, *Political Economy and Capitalism* (London, 1937).

R. PALME DUTT, *Fascism and Social Revolution* (London, 1934).

DIETRICH EICHHOLZ and KURT GOSSWEILER, 'Noch einmal: Politik und Wirtschaft, 1933–1945', *Das Argument*, 47 (1968).

RENÉ ERBE, *Die nationalsozialistische Wirtschaftspolitik 1933–1939 im Lichte der modernen Theorie* (Zurich, 1958).

E. H. ERIKSON, 'Hitler's Imagery and German Youth', *Psychiatry*, vol. 4 (November 1942).

J. EVOLA, *Il fascismo* (Rome, 1964).

*Fascism in Europe*, 2 vols (Prague, 1969–70).

R. DE FELICE, *Storia degli ebrei italiani sotto il fascismo* (Turin, 1961).

——, *Il fascismo. Le interpretazioni dei contemporanei e degli storici* (Bari, 1970).

——, *Le interpretazioni del fascismo* (Bari, 1974).

——, *Mussolini il rivoluzionario (1883–1920)* (Turin, 1965).

——, *Mussolini il fascista. La conquista del potere (1921–1925)* (Turin, 1966).

——, *Mussolini il fascista. L'organizzazione dello stato fascista (1925–1929)* (Turin, 1968).

OTTO FENICHEL, 'Psychoanalysis of Anti-semitism', *American Imago*, I, 2 (1940).

F. FERRY (ed.), *Lo stato operaio 1927–1939* (Rome, 1964).

WOLFRAM FISCHER, *Die Wirtschaftspolitik des Nazionalsozialismus* (Lüneberg, 1961).

M. T. FLORINSKY, *Fascism and National Socialism: A Study of the Economic and Social Policies of the Totalitarian State* (New York, 1936).

MICHEL FOUCAULT, ALAIN GEISMAR and ANDRÉ GLUCKSMANN, *Neuer Faschismus, neue Demokratie* (Berlin, 1972).

E. FRAENKEL, *The Dual State* (New York, 1941).

C. J. FRIEDRICH, *Totalitarianism* (Cambridge, Mass., 1945).

—— and Z. K. BRZEZINSKI, *Totalitarian Dictatorship and Autocracy* (New York, 1956).

——, MICHAEL CURTIS and BENJAMIN R. BARBER, *Totalitarianism in Perspective* (New York, 1969).

ERICH FROMM, *Escape from Freedom* (New York, 1941).

A. GRAMSCI, *L'Ordine Nuovo, 1919–1920* (Turin, 1955).

——, *Socialismo e fascismo* (Turin, 1966).

HELGA GREBING, *Aktuelle Theorien über Faschismus und Konservatismus. Eine Kritik* (Stuttgart, 1974).

——, *Der Nationalsozialismus. Ursprung und Wesen* (Munich, 1964).

M. GREIFFENHAGEN, R. KÜHNL and J. B. MÜLLER, *Totalitarismus* (Munich, 1972).

RÜDIGER GRIEPENBURG and K. H. TJADEN, 'Faschismus und Bonapartismus. Zur Kritik der Faschismustheorie August Thalheimers', *Das Argument*, 41 (1966).

DIETER GROSSER, 'Die nationalsozialistische Wirtschaft. Die deutsche Industrie und die Nationalsozialisten', *Das Argument*, 32 (1965).

A. GROTH, 'The "isms" in Totalitarianism', *American Political Science Review*, vol. 58, no. 4 (1964).

E. GRÜNBERG, *Der Mittelstand in der kapitalistischen Gesellschaft* (Leipzig, 1932).

DANIEL GUERIN, *Sur le Fascisme* (Paris, 1971).

C. HAIDER, *Capital and Labour under Fascism* (New York, 1930).

G. W. F. HALLGARTEN, *Hitler, Reichswehr und Industrie* (Frankfurt, 1955).

A. HAMILTON, *The Appeal of Fascism* (London, 1971).

W. F. HAUG, *Der Hilflose Antifaschismus* (Frankfurt, 1970).

KLAUS HILDEBRAND, *Vom Reich zur Weltreich. Hitler N.S.D.A.P. und koloniale Frage 1919–1945* (Munich, 1969).

MAX HORKHEIMER, 'Die Juden und Europa', *Studies in Philosophy and Social Science*, vol. VIII (1939).

——, *Studien über Autorität und Familie* (Paris, 1936).

——, *Traditionelle und kritische Theorie* (Frankfurt, 1970).

H. HUSS and A. SCHRÖDER, *Antisemitismus. Zur Pathologie der burgerlichen Gesellschaft* (Frankfurt, 1965).

MARTIN JAY, *The Dialectical Imagination* (London, 1973).

MICHAEL H. KATER, 'Zur Soziographie der frühen N.S.D.A.P.', *Vierteljahreshefte für Zeitgeschichte*, 19 (1971).

MARTIN KITCHEN, 'August Thalheimer's Theory of Fascism', *Journal of the History of Ideas*, vol. XXXIV, no. 1 (1974).

——, 'Ernst Nolte and the Phenomenology of Fascism', *Science and Society*, 2 (1974).

——, 'Trotsky's Theory of Fascism', *Social Praxis* (1975).

FRITZ KLEIN, 'Zur Vorbereitung der faschistischen Diktatur durch die deutsche Grossbourgeoisie', *Zeitschrift für Geschichtswissenschaft*, 1 (1953).

ERNST KRISS, 'The Covenant of Gangsters', *Psychiatry Digest*, 4 (1943).

REINHARD KÜHNL, *Deutschland zwischen Demokratie und Faschismus* (Munich, 1969).

——, *Formen bürgerlicher Herrschaft, Liberalismus–Faschismus* (Hamburg, 1971).

——, *Die nationalsozialistische Linke, 1925–1930* (Meisenheim, 1966).

——, *Texte zur Faschismusdiskussion* (Hamburg, 1974).

AXEL KUHN, *Das faschistische Herrschaftssystem und die moderne Gesellschaft* (Hamburg, 1973).

——, *Hitlers aussenpolitisches Programm* (Stuttgart, 1970).

A. LABRIOLA, *Le due politiche. Fascismo e riformismo* (Naples, 1923).

WALTER LAQUEUR and GEORGE L. MOSSE, *International Fascism* (New York, 1966).

HAROLD LASKI, *Reflections on the Revolution in Our Time* (London, 1943).

HAROLD LASSWELL, 'The Psychology of Hitlerism', *Political Quarterly*, 4 (1933).

Bibliography 97

E. LEDERER, *The State of the Masses* (New York, 1940).

KARL O. LESSKER, 'Who Voted for Hitler? A New Look at the Class Basis of Naziism', *American Journal of Sociology*, 74 (1968).

E. LEWIN, 'Zum Faschismusanalyse durch die kommunistischen Internationale', *Beiträge zur Geschichte der deutschen Arbeiterbewegung*, 1 (1970).

SEYMOUR MARTIN LIPSET, 'Der "Faschismus", die Linke, die Rechte und die Mitte', *Kölner Zeitschrift für Soziologie und Sozialpsychologie*, 11 (1959).

PETER LOEWENBERG, 'The Unsuccessful Adolescence of Heinrich Himmler', *American Historical Review*, 76, 3 (June 1971).

——, 'The Psychohistorical Origins of the Nazi Youth Cohort', *American Historical Review*, 76, 5 (December 1971).

RUDOLPH M. LOEWENSTEIN, *Psychoanalyse des Antisemitismus* (Frankfurt, 1971).

B. R. LOPUKHOV, 'Il problema del fascismo italiano negli scritti di autori sovietici', *Studi Storici* (April/June 1965).

G. LUKACS, *Die Zerstörung der Vernunft*, 3 vols (Neuwied, 1973/4).

H. C. F. MANSILLA, *Faschismus und eindimensionelle Gesellschaft* (Neuwied, 1971).

A. H. MASLOW, 'The Authoritarian Character Structure', *Journal of Social Psychology*, 18 (1943).

TIM MASON, 'Der Primat der Politik – Politik und Wirtschaft im Nationalsozialismus', *Das Argument*, 41 (1966).

——, 'Primat der Industrie? – Eine Erwiderung', *Das Argument*, 47 (1968).

R. MICHELS, *Sozialismus und Faschismus in Italien* (Munich, 1925).

RALPH MILIBAND, *The State in Capitalist Society* (London, 1969).

DIETFRIED MÜLLER-HEGEMANN, *Zur Psychologie des deutschen Faschisten* (Rudolstadt, 1955).

FRANZ NEUMANN, *Behemoth: The Structure and Practice of National Socialism* (London, 1942).

——, *The Democratic and the Authoritarian State* (New York, 1957).

SIGMUND NEUMANN, *Permanent Revolution* (London, 1965).

F. S. NITTI, *Bolscevismo, Fascismo e Democrazia* (New York, 1927).

ERNST NOLTE, *The Three Faces of Fascism* (London, 1965).

——, *Die Krise des liberalen Systems und die faschistischen Bewegungen* (Munich, 1968).

——, *Theorien über den Faschismus* (Cologne, 1970).

R. PARIS, *Histoire du fascisme en Italie* (Paris, 1962).

——, *Les Origines du fascisme* (Paris, 1969).

TALCOTT PARSONS, *Essays in Sociological Theory* (New York, 1949).

DIETER PETZINA, 'Hitler und die deutsche Industrie. Ein kommentierter Literatur- und Forschungsbericht', *Geschichte in Wissenschaft und Unterricht*, 17 (1966).

WILHELM PIECK, GEORGI DIMITROFF and PALMIRO TOGLIATTI, *Die Offensive des Faschismus und die Aufgaben der Kommunisten in Kampf für die Volksfront gegen Krieg und Faschismus. Referate auf dem VII. Kongress der Kommunistischen Internationale 1935* (Berlin, 1957).

THEO PIRKER, *Komintern und Faschismus. Dokumente zur Geschichte und Theorie des Faschismus* (Stuttgart, 1965).

G. PISCHEL, *Il problemo dei ceti medi* (Milan, 1946).

NICOS POULANTZAS, *Fascism and Dictatorship* (London, 1974).

N. S. PRESTON, *Politics, Economics and Power: Ideology and Practice under Capitalism, Socialism, Communism and Fascism* (New York, 1967).

KAREN PRIESTER, *Der italienische Faschismus. Oekonomische und ideologische Grundlagen* (Cologne, 1972).

S. RANULF, *Moral Indignation and Middle-class Psychology* (Copenhagen, 1938).

WILHELM REICH, *The Mass Psychology of Fascism* (New York, 1946).

ERNST-AUGUST ROLOFF, 'Wer wählte Hitler? Thesen zur Sozial- und Wirtschaftsgeschichte der Weimarer Republik', *Politische Studien*, 15 (1964).

R. ROMEO, *Breve storia della grande industria in Italia* (Rome, 1967).

——, *Risorgimento e capitalismo* (Rome, 1959).

L. ROSENSTOCK-FRANCK, *L'Economie corporative fasciste en doctrine et en fait* (Paris, 1934).

L. SALVATORELLI, *Nazionalfascismo* (Turin, 1923).

——, *Pensiero e azione del risorgimento* (Rome, 1944).

G. SALVEMINI, *The Fascist Dictatorship in Italy* (London, 1928).

D. J. SAPOSS, 'The Role of the Middle Class in Social Development: Fascism, Populism, Communism, Socialism', in *Economic Essays in Honor of Wesley Clair Mitchell* (New York, 1935).

WOLFGANG SAUER, 'National Socialism: Totalitarianism or Fascism?', *American Historical Review*, 73 (1967).

RAYMOND DE SAUSSURE, 'Collective Neurosis of Germany', *Free World*, v (February 1943).

——, 'L'Inconnu chez Hitler', *Les Oeuvres Nouvelles* (New York, 1943).

——, 'Psychopathology of Adolf Hitler', *Free World*, III (July 1942).

C. T. SCHMIDT, *The Corporative State in Action: Italy under Fascism* (New York, 1939).

H. W. SCHNEIDER, *Making the Fascist State* (New York, 1928).

DAVID SCHOENBAUM, *Hitler's Social Revolution* (New York, 1966).

OTTO-ERNST SCHÜDDEKOPF, *Fascism* (London, 1973).

ARTHUR SCHWEITZER, *Big Business in the Third Reich* (Bloomington, Ind., 1965).

I. SILONE, *Der Faschismus* (Zürich, 1934).

P. SPRIANO, 'L'esperienza di Tasca e Mosca e il "socialfascismo"', *Studi Storici*, I (1969).

J. L. TALMON, *The Origins of Totalitarian Democracy* (London, 1952).

ANGELO TASCA, *The Rise of Italian Fascism, 1918–1922* (New York, 1966).

PALMIRO TOGLIATTI, 'A proposito del fascismo', *Società* (Dec 1952).

——, *La formazione del gruppo dirigente del partito communista italiano nel 1923–1924* (Rome, 1962).

——, *Lezioni sul fascismo* (Rome, 1970).

——, *Opere*, I (Rome, 1967).

C. TREVES, *Il fascismo nella literatura antifascistica dell'esilio* (Rome, 1953).

W. TROTTER, *Instincts of the Herd in Peace and War* (London, 1919).

F. TURATI, *Le problème du fascisme au congrès international socialiste* (Brussels, 1928).

HENRY ASHBY TURNER JR, 'Big Business and the Rise of Hitler', *American Historical Review*, 75 (1969).

MARTIN WANGH, 'Psychoanalytische Betrachtungen zur Dynamik und Genese des Vorurteils, des Antisemitismus und des Nazismus', *Psyche*, V, 16 (5) (1962).

EUGEN WEBER, *Varieties of Fascism: Doctrines of Revolution in the Twentieth Century* (London, 1964).

ANDREW WHITESIDE, 'The Nature and Origins of National Socialism', *Journal of Central European Affairs*, 17 (1957).

W. G. WELK, *Fascist Economic Policy* (Cambridge, Mass., 1938).

H. A. WINKLER, *Mittelstand, Demokratie und Nationalsozialismus* (Cologne, 1972).

ELIZABETH WISKEMANN, *Fascism in Italy* (London, 1969).

S. J. WOOLF (ed.), *European Fascism* (London, 1970).

——, *The Nature of Fascism* (London, 1968).

# Index